D1597801

GARY E. WITTLICH · LEE HUMPHRIES

EAR TRAINING

An Approach through Music Literature

EAR TRAINING

An Approach through Music Literature

GARY E. WITTLICH

Indiana University

LEE HUMPHRIES

University of Minnesota

HARCOURT BRACE JOVANOVICH, INC.

New York   Chicago   San Francisco   Atlanta

© 1974 by Harcourt Brace Jovanovich, Inc.

ISBN: 0-15-518707-4

Library of Congress Card Number: 74-10422

Printed in the United States of America

PREFACE

This book approaches ear training through the study of complete musical works. Its premise is that the musical ear develops through the study of *music*—actual musical compositions, not out-of-context excerpts or brief exercises composed for teaching purposes. *Ear Training* is designed to be used by itself in freshman ear-training classes or in conjunction with a theory text in classes that combine ear training with other aspects of elementary theory. Units 1 to 10 presuppose only a knowledge of intervals, scales, key signatures, triads and seventh chords, and basic notational skills. Units 11 to 14 are more advanced, but even in these units most of the materials can be used in freshman classes.

At the heart of the book are fourteen complete works or movements from the music of the fifteenth to the twentieth century, works chosen to provide a careful balance of length, complexity, performing medium, genre, and formal structure. A full score of each work is included in the book, and a two-record set of all the selections is available from the publisher. These fourteen works are the source of a variety of questions, self-drills, and dictation exercises organized with the purpose of leading students to a thorough understanding of each work as a whole in terms of its musical materials and their interrelationships. That understanding is the end toward which ear training is a means; that understanding is the reason for this book.

Each unit begins with a brief historical-stylistic note about the work in that unit and a list of terms used in the unit that students may need to check in the Glossary. All units then continue with the following three sections:

General Questions. These questions are arranged in four groups. Groups 1 to 3 each deal with rhythm, pitch, texture, and form and are to be answered by *listening only*, without reference to the score. The three groups are structured so that the questions in Group 1 are simpler than those in Group 2, and those in Group 2 simpler than those in Group 3; similarly, to the extent possible, the questions within each group progress from less detailed to more detailed considerations. Answers to all questions in these three groups appear at the end of the book. The questions in Group 4 are concerned with score reading and analysis, their purpose being to provide a point of departure for classroom discussion.

Practice Drills. Here students are asked to tap pitchless rhythmic patterns and to sing and play arhythmic pitch patterns from the work. Again, the order in each category is from simpler to more difficult. Also included for singing, playing, and analysis are some of the sonority types (mostly triads and seventh chords) and chord patterns (mostly cadential) that are prominent in the work. These self-drills have several purposes: they provide extensive practice in sight reading; they get the basic materials of the work into the students' ears; and they prepare the way for the more demanding dictation exercises that follow. Measure numbers are provided throughout the drills for self-checking in the score.

Dictation and Analysis.   In this section, students are asked to notate rhythmic excerpts, arhythmic pitch patterns, melodic excerpts, contrapuntal passages in two or more voices, and the outer voices of harmonic progressions. For all these exercises, lead-in notes and rests are included. Some of the melodic and contrapuntal excerpts are presented in both their original version and in a reduced, simplified version that can serve as a conceptual link to later studies in Schenkerian-Salzerian analysis. Students are also asked to identify chords either by sonority type, numeral function, or function class. (The concept of chord function class is simple, but it may be new to some instructors. Essentially, it reduces chord functions to three classes: tonic, pre-dominant, and dominant. With this classification, beginning students are spared the difficulty of identifying certain secondary dominants and other chromatic chords by specific numeral function. Compare the Glossary entries "chord function" and "chord function class" for more detail.) The Selective Listening exercises in this section ask students to listen for certain special features in the work, such as the types of cadences, nonchord tones, and tonal changes.

Obviously, this arrangement allows for great flexibility. The units are arranged chronologically, but they may be taken up in any order in a variety of ways. One instructor may choose to work straight through all the material within each unit. Another may want to assign Group 1 of the General Questions in all units as an introductory overview. Still another may decide to produce a rhythm module by concentrating on the rhythm questions, rhythm drills, and rhythm dictation exercises of several selected units. These are only a few of the possibilities. Even the index increases the flexibility of the book in its design as a special teaching aid. The instructor who wishes to discuss some particular topic—cross relations, orchestration, or secondary dominants, for example—can consult the index for a list of the questions and exercises in all units where the topic applies, whether or not the term itself is mentioned in the text.

The book works equally well in and out of the classroom. All the dictation exercises are available on tapes from the publisher for independent student work, but these exercises are also included in full in a piano version at the end of the book, keyed by measure numbers, for instructors who wish to play them in class. The book is perforated for optional tear-out assignments, but its layout is planned so that the fourteen scores and their headnotes will remain intact as an anthology for later use in music literature and analysis courses.

It is difficult to acknowledge all those who have contributed to this book, but the authors would like to thank especially Allen Winold of Indiana University, whose advice and critical insights into the nature of music teaching have been invaluable; Richard Domek of the University of Kentucky, whose classroom testing of some of the materials was very helpful; and Burdette Green of The Ohio State University, whose review of the first draft of the manuscript was of great assistance in shaping the final version. In addition, we thank our theory colleagues at both Indiana University and the University of Minnesota for their encouragement.

G. E. W.
L. H.

CONTENTS

JOHN DUNSTABLE
(c.1385–1452)

Quam pulcra es

John Dunstable was a noted English mathematician and astrologer, in addition to being one of the most famous composers of the fifteenth century. His musical influence extended to the continent, where Dufay, Binchois, and other composers of the Burgundian School followed his lead in subordinating counterpoint to triadic harmony.

Quam pulcra es is a motet—a short, usually unaccompanied vocal work on a sacred text, and the most important form of early polyphonic music. Here, the text is a setting of selected verses from the seventh chapter of the Biblical *Song of Solomon:*

> How fair and pleasant you are, O loved one, delectable maiden! You are stately as a palm tree, and your breasts are like its clusters. Your head crowns you like Carmel. . . . Your neck is like an ivory tower. Come, my beloved, let us go forth into the fields . . . and see whether the grape blossoms have opened and the pomegranates are in bloom. There will I give you my love.

Throughout the work the textual rhythm controls the rhythm of the music, and at one point the word *veni* ("come") is highlighted by long, sustained tones. The crossing of voices is characteristic of the period, as is the standardization of cadences.

Note to the student: Editions of early music vary, be prepared for slight variations in the recording you hear for this work.

GENERAL QUESTIONS

TERMS

Before beginning this unit, make sure you know the meaning of each of the following terms. Check the Glossary at the end of the book for any term that is unfamiliar to you.

RHYTHM   hemiola

PITCH   modal cadences (Ionian cadence, Dorian cadence, Phrygian cadence, Lydian cadence, double leading-tone cadence, under-third cadence), cross relation, $\frac{8}{5}$ sonority

TEXTURE   points of imitation, text setting (syllabic, neumatic, melismatic), contrary motion, oblique motion, similar motion

GROUP 1

RHYTHM

1. This work falls into two main sections, the second of which is (slower)(faster) than the first.

2. The meter of the work is
   a. $\frac{3}{4}$ b. $\frac{6}{8}$ c. $\frac{3}{4}$ with some feeling of $\frac{6}{8}$

PITCH

1. The pitch material is
   a. diatonic   b. chromatic   c. diatonic with occasional chromaticism

2. During the course of this composition the tonal center (does)(does not) change.

TEXTURE

1. How many vocal lines are there?
   a. two   b. three   c. four   d. more than four

2. All voices (occasionally)(frequently) articulate the same syllable of text at the same time.

FORM

1. The subsections that can be heard within the two main sections are delineated by
   a. changes of register   b. changes of dynamics   c. rests

2. The length of the phrases (does)(does not) vary.

GROUP 2

RHYTHM

1. A sixteenth note is the shortest value used. Which of the following statements best describes its appearance?
   a. Series of sixteenth notes appear in scalar passages.
   b. Sixteenth notes appear only in the approach to cadences.
   c. Sixteenth notes appear in the recurring rhythmic motive ♩. ♫

2. Which of the following statements best describes the rhythmic relationship of the lines to each other?
   a. The lines move in the same rhythm.
   b. The lines move in contrasting rhythms.
   c. Sometimes the lines move in the same rhythm, while at other times they move in contrasting rhythms.

PITCH

1. The upper line consists of
   a. seconds with occasional thirds
   b. seconds and thirds
   c. seconds and thirds with occasional fourths and fifths

2. Which of the following sonorities is used at most cadences in this work?

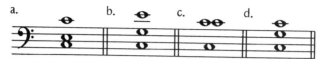

3. Which of the following patterns represents the upper voice's approach to the final cadence?

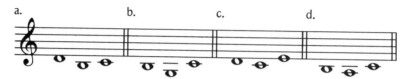

TEXTURE

1. Which of the following statements best describes the role of imitation in this work?
   a. There is no imitation.
   b. There are brief hints of imitation.
   c. The work is based on points of imitation.

2. At cadences the outer voices generally move in
   a. expanding contrary motion
   b. contracting contrary motion
   c. similar motion
   d. oblique motion

FORM

Which of the following statements best describes the conclusion of the work?
   a. There is an exact return to the opening thematic material.
   b. There is a modified return to the opening thematic material.
   c. There is no return to the opening thematic material.

GROUP 3

RHYTHM

1. The opening rhythm of the upper voice is

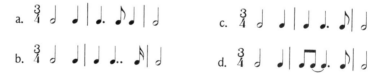

2. At the beginning of the second main section the upper voice has a rhythmic figure that
   a. is exactly like its rhythm at the opening of the work
   b. is a modification of its rhythm at the opening of the work
   c. has no relation to its rhythm at the opening of the work

PITCH

1. Which of the following patterns represents the opening pitch material of the upper voice?

2. Which of the following sonorities rarely appear(s) in this work?

    a. M$^6_4$ b. o$^6_3$ c. m$^6_4$ d. M$^5_3$ e. m$^5_3$

3. Which of the following items appear(s) in the work?

    a. repeated notes   d. under-third cadence
    b. cross relation   e. suspension
    c. double leading-tone cadence

TEXTURE

1. The distance between the outer voices is never greater than

    a. an octave   b. a perfect twelfth   c. two octaves

2. The text setting is

    a. syllabic   c. melismatic
    b. neumatic   d. syllabic with melismatic approaches to cadences

FORM

As you listen, write under each lettered bracket in the diagram below the number of the appropriate musical event:

(1) change of tempo
(2) a passage primarily based on parallel first-inversion triads
(3) sustained chords emphasizing the word *veni*
(4) a momentary feeling of $\frac{3}{2}$ meter resulting from a hemiola rhythm
(5) subsectional division created by a measure of silence
(6) a melisma on the word *alleluia*
(7) imitation

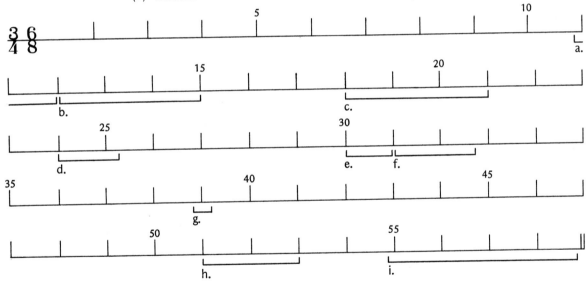

GROUP 4

**SCORE
STUDY
AND
DISCUSSION**

1. Examine the intervallic structure of each voice. Can instances of triadic influence be found? How do the voices differ? How do you account for these differences?

2. Locate examples of imitation. (Some have already been pointed out to you.) At what interval from the original figure do the answering voices enter? What is the distance in time between each original figure and its imitations?

3. Locate important cadences. What tonic is heard at each? Plot the various tonics of the work on the staff below. Which receive(s) greatest emphasis?

PRACTICE DRILLS

RHYTHM

Tap or intone each of the following rhythmic patterns. Then play them on your instrument, being sure to give all notes their full value. (Perform two-line patterns either with another student or at the piano, playing one line while tapping or intoning the other, then reversing the procedure.)

1. (mm. 35-38)

2. (mm. 55-58)

3. (mm. 55-58)

4. (mm. 19-22)

PITCH PATTERNS

Sing each of the following nonrhythmicized pitch-pattern excerpts, transposing up or down an octave as necessary to accommodate your voice range. Then play them on your instrument to check your accuracy.

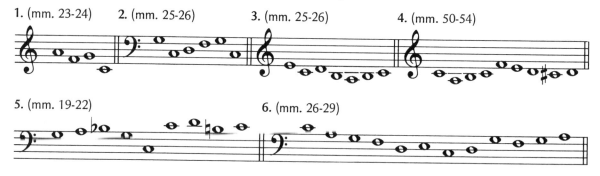

1. (mm. 23-24)   2. (mm. 25-26)   3. (mm. 25-26)   4. (mm. 50-54)

5. (mm. 19-22)   6. (mm. 26-29)

SONORITY TYPES

Play each of the following sonorities at the piano and sing each tone while the sonority is sounding. Play each sonority again, leaving out one of the tones; sing the missing tone. Repeat this procedure with each of the other tones.

Sing the sonority from the bass up and from the soprano down, using a close spacing to accommodate your voice range.

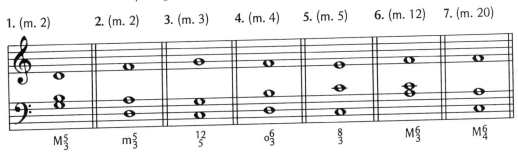

CHORD PROGRESSIONS

At the piano, play the chord progressions given on the bottom two staves while singing the vocalises given on the top staff. If you are not a keyboard player, arpeggiate the progressions on your instrument.

Without the aid of the piano, sing the vocalises and the progressions from the bass up and from the soprano down.

Analyze each progression by numeral as specifically as possible in terms of the tonal center given for it.

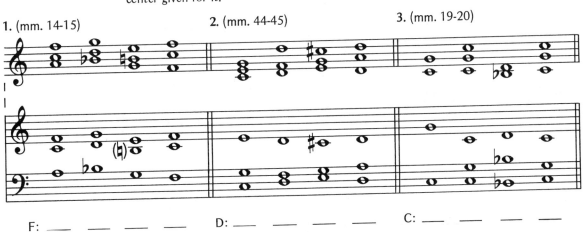

DICTATION AND ANALYSIS

RHYTHM

You will hear one- and two-part excerpts from the work. Notate the *rhythm only* of each excerpt. For each, the number of voice parts, the basic duration, and the suggested number of hearings, respectively, are given in parentheses.

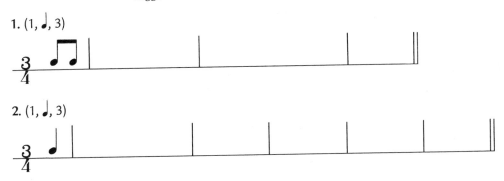

3. (1, ♩ and ♩., 3)

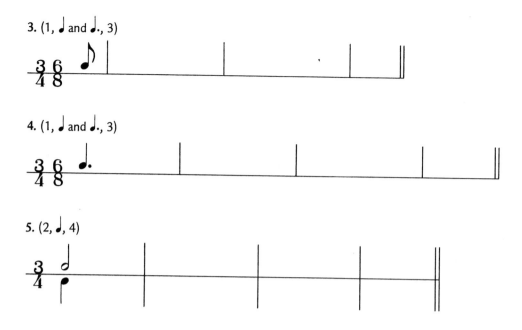

4. (1, ♩ and ♩., 3)

5. (2, ♩, 4)

PITCH PATTERNS

Notate in whole notes the nonrhythmicized pitch-pattern excerpts that will be played for you. The suggested number of hearings is given in parentheses.

1. (2) **2.** (2) **3.** (2) **4.** (3)

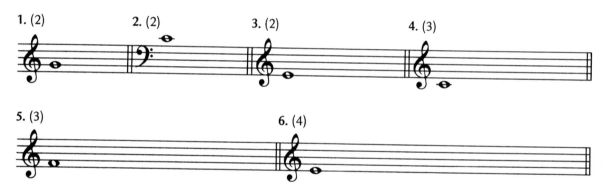

5. (3) **6.** (4)

MELODIES

The melodies in this section are presented in two versions: (A) is a *basic* melody—that is, a reduced version of the original melody—and (B) is the *original* melody. Notate the basic melody on staff A and the original melody on staff B. The suggested number of hearings is given in parentheses. (For the original melody, this number is based on your having completed the basic melody first.)

1. (2)

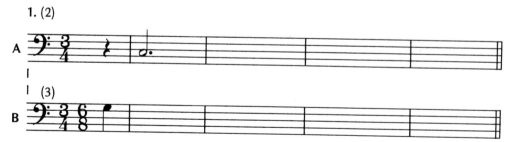

COUNTERPOINT

The exercises in this section are presented in two versions: (A) is a *basic* counterpoint—that is, a reduced version of the original passage—and (B) is the *original* counterpoint. Notate the basic counterpoint on staff A and the original counterpoint on staff B. The suggested number of hearings is given in parentheses. (For the original version, this number is based on your having completed the basic version first.)

1.

2.

SONORITY TYPES

Each of the following items represents a sonority that you are to identify in two hearings. The number of voices in each sonority is three.

You are given the highest (stem up) or the lowest (stem down) pitch for each sonority. Notate the other outer voice and as many of the inner voices as you can. Be sure to include any necessary accidentals.

Below each sonority, indicate its sounding chord quality, including inversion (for example, m_4^6, M_3^5, Mm_3^6, $\frac{8}{5}$).

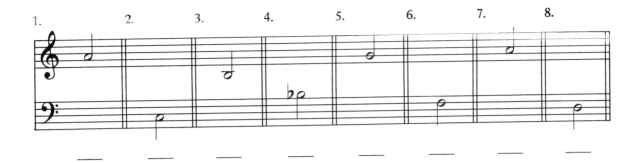

SELECTIVE LISTENING

NONCHORD TONES

In the following exercises you are given the rhythm of the outer voices of excerpts from the work. Each contains nonchord tones, the location of which is indicated by asterisks. From the following list, select the appropriate nonchord tone and place its letter beside the corresponding asterisk. The suggested number of hearings for each exercise is two.

a. anticipation   c. passing tone   e. double suspension
b. neighbor tone   d. suspension   f. escape tone

TONAL CHANGE

You will hear two harmonic progressions in which tonal changes occur. For each, the first tonic is given. Add the letter names of the other tonics. Two hearings are suggested for the first excerpt; three for the second.

1. First tonic: C   second tonic: _____

2. First tonic: D   second tonic: _____   third tonic: _____

CADENCE TYPES	You will hear two excerpts from the work. From the following list, select the appropriate cadence for each excerpt. The suggested number of hearings is two.

a. Ionian (vii°$_6$-I$^8_5$)   c. Phrygian (♭vii$_6$-i$^8_5$)

b. Dorian (♭VII$_6$-i$^8_5$)   d. Lydian (or double leading tone) (vii$_6$-I$^8_5$)

HARMONIC PROGRESSIONS

1. Below you are given the first pitch of the outer voices and the harmonic rhythm of a harmonic progression. Notate the outer voices and place an "X" under each first-inversion triad. The suggested number of hearings is five.

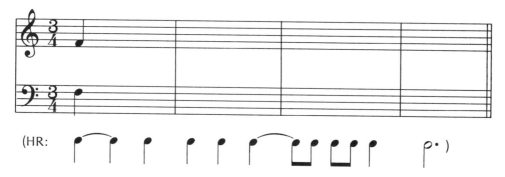

2. Below you are given the first pitch of the outer voices and the harmonic rhythm of a harmonic progression. Notate the outer voices and place an "X" under each $^6_8$ sonority. The suggested number of hearings is five.

3. Below you are given the first pitch of the outer voices and the harmonic rhythm of a harmonic progression. The chord vocabulary consists only of triads built on the tonic and on the leading tone. Notate the outer voices and place an "X" under each vii°$_6$. The suggested number of hearings is five.

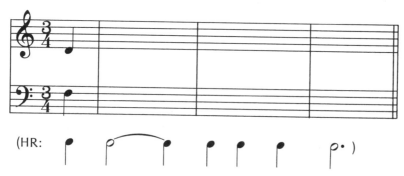

JOSQUIN DES PREZ
(c.1450–1521)

Gloria
from MISSA PANGE LINGUA

Missa Pange lingua, published posthumously in 1539, is thought to be one of Josquin's late masses. The work is an example of a *paraphrase mass,* in which an existing melody—often, as here, a Gregorian chant (plainsong)—was borrowed, "paraphrased" by means of melodic and rhythmic altera-tions, and embedded in the new melodic material. In earlier masses this treatment was applied only to the upper voice, but in *Missa Pange lingua* (which Gustave Reese calls "a fantasy on a plainsong") the chant appears in all four voices. This mass is cited by Willi Apel as probably the earliest example of a complete paraphrase mass.

The "Gloria" is the second item in the Ordinary of the Mass, following the "Kyrie." Here is a translation of the text, the first phrase of which is traditionally intoned by the priest:

> Glory be to God in the highest. And on earth peace to men of good will. We praise Thee. We bless Thee. We adore Thee. We glorify Thee. We give Thee thanks for Thy great glory. O Lord God, heavenly King, God the Father almighty. O Lord Jesus Christ, the only-begotten Son. Lord God, Lamb of God, Son of the Father. Who taketh away the sins of the world, have mercy upon us. Who taketh away the sins of the world, receive our prayer. Who sitteth at the right hand of the Father, have mercy upon us. For Thou alone art holy. Thou alone art Lord. Thou alone, O Jesus Christ, art most high. Together with the Holy Ghost, in the glory of God the Father. Amen.

Note to the student: Editions of early music vary; be prepared for slight variations in the recording you hear for this work.

14   JOSQUIN: GLORIA

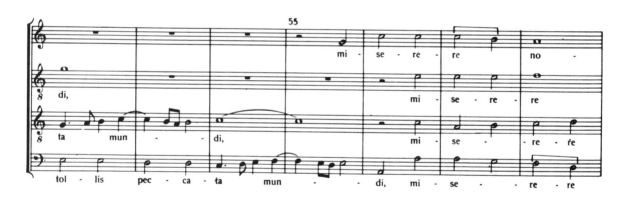

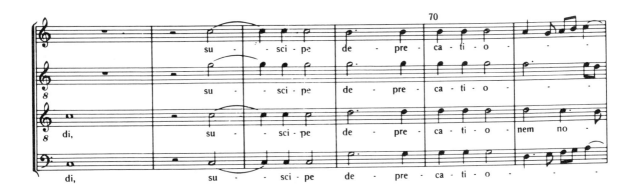

GENERAL QUESTIONS

TERMS

Before beginning this unit, make sure you know the meaning of each of the following terms. Check the Glossary at the end of the book for any term that is unfamiliar to you.

RHYTHM	composite rhythm, rhythmic density
PITCH	modal cadences (double leading-tone cadence, under-third cadence), root movement, nonchord tones, $\frac{8}{5}$ sonority
TEXTURE	points of imitation, text setting (syllabic, neumatic, melismatic)

GROUP 1

RHYTHM

1. The meter (does)(does not) change within this work.

2. With ♩ as the basic duration, the shortest rhythmic value used is

    a. ♩   b. ♪.   c. ♪   d. ♬

PITCH

1. The melodic organization is

    a. nonmotivic
    b. based on recurring motives
    c. based on nonrecurring motives

2. The pitch material is

    a. diatonic   b. chromatic   c. diatonic with occasional chromaticism

TEXTURE

1. The texture is

    a. chordal   b. contrapuntal   c. a mixture of chordal and contrapuntal

2. How many voice parts are there?

    a. two   b. three   c. four   d. more than four

FORM

1. How many main sections are there?

    a. two   b. three   c. four   d. five

2. The immediate repetition of phrases is an (important)(unimportant) aspect of the formal procedure.

GROUP 2

RHYTHM

1. In the first main section the meter is

    a. $\frac{3}{2}$ with some feeling of $\frac{6}{4}$ b. $\frac{3}{2}$ c. $\frac{6}{4}$ d. $\frac{2}{2}$

2. In the second main section the meter is

    a. $\frac{3}{2}$ with some feeling of $\frac{6}{4}$ b. $\frac{3}{2}$ c. $\frac{6}{4}$ d. $\frac{2}{2}$

3. Throughout the work the harmonic rhythm

    a. is consistent   b. varies

PITCH

1. Which of the following nonchord tones is the principal dissonance used?

    a. appoggiatura   c. anticipation
    b. suspension   d. neighbor tone

2. The final sonority is a/an

    a. major triad   b. minor triad   c. octave   d. $\frac{8}{5}$ sonority

TEXTURE

1. Lengthy (duet)(trio) passages are prominently employed.

2. Which of the following statements best describes the role of imitation in this work?

    a. There is no imitation.
    b. There are brief hints of imitation.
    c. The work is based on points of imitation.

FORM

1. The second main section begins with

    a. the opening motive of the work
    b. a modification of the opening motive of the work
    c. a new motive

2. Which of the following is/are used to create subsections?

    a. change of rhythmic density   d. alteration of the phrase length
    b. introduction of a new motive   e. change of vocal timbre
    c. momentary cessation of rhythmic activity

GROUP 3

RHYTHM

1. The rhythm of the opening motive is

2. Which of the following does not/do not represent a treatment of the eighth note in this work?

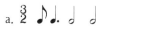  

PITCH

1. The opening motive is answered by an imitative entry lying

    a. a perfect fourth lower   c. a minor sixth lower
    b. a perfect fifth lower   d. a major sixth lower

2. Which of the following patterns represents the entering pitches of the soprano, alto, tenor, and bass at the beginning of the second section, "Qui tollis"?

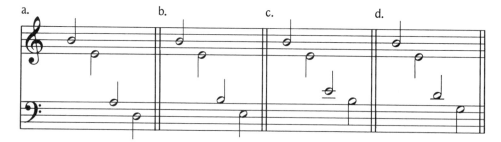

3. The root movement at the final cadence is

    a. down a minor third   c. up a perfect fourth
    b. up a major second   d. up a perfect fifth

4. Which of the cadences listed below does not/do not appear in this work?

    a. V-i cadence   b. double leading-tone cadence   c. under-third cadence

TEXTURE

1. The text setting is

    a. syllabic   b. neumatic   c. melismatic   d. a balance of (a), (b), and (c)

2. The work (does)(does not) contain passages where two voices move in parallel intervals for two or more beats.

FORM

As you listen, write under each lettered bracket in the diagram below the number of the appropriate musical event:

(1) meter change from $\frac{3}{2}$ to ¢

(2) four imitative entries at the octave or unison

(3) composite rhythm moving in ♩'s

(4) under-third cadence

(5) repetition of the preceding material

(6) passage based on the repetition of a motive and a harmonic progression

(7) chordal texture, slow harmonic rhythm, and syllabic text setting

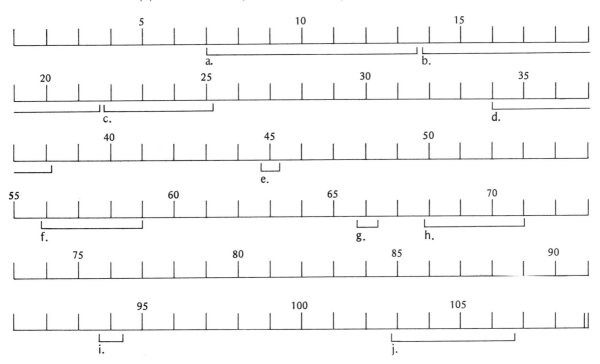

GROUP 4

SCORE STUDY AND DISCUSSION

1. The Gregorian plainsong *Pange lingua* on which this mass is based is quoted below. Trace its appearance in each of the vocal lines. Do some portions of the chant receive greater emphasis than others?

2. Examine the cadences in this work. How are they created? Do all the voices cadence together? What kind of dissonance is frequently associated with the cadences? By what kind of motion is the cadential interval or sonority approached? What harmonic functions do you hear?

PRACTICE DRILLS

RHYTHM

Tap or intone each of the following rhythmic patterns. Then play them on your instrument, being sure to give all notes their full value. (Perform two-line patterns either with another student or at the piano, playing one line while tapping or intoning the other, then reversing the procedure.)

1. (mm. 45-50)

2. (mm. 74-78)

3. (mm. 91-94)

4. (mm. 36-38)

PITCH PATTERNS

Sing each of the following nonrhythmicized pitch-pattern excerpts, transposing up or down an octave as necessary to accommodate your voice range. Then play them on your instrument to check your accuracy.

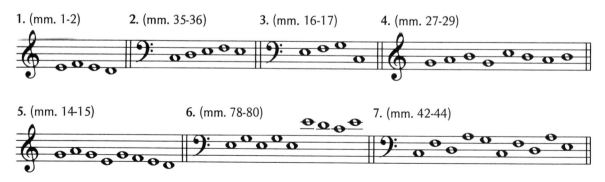

1. (mm. 1-2)   **2.** (mm. 35-36)   **3.** (mm. 16-17)   **4.** (mm. 27-29)

5. (mm. 14-15)   **6.** (mm. 78-80)   **7.** (mm. 42-44)

Play each of the following sonorities at the piano and sing each tone while the sonority is sounding. Play each sonority again, leaving out one of the tones; sing the missing tone. Repeat this procedure with each of the other tones.

Sing the sonority from the bass up and from the soprano down, using a close spacing to accommodate your voice range.

1. (m. 16) **2.** (m. 28) **3.** (m. 71) **4.** (m. 67) **5.** (m. 69) **6.** (m. 104) **7.** (m. 45) **8.** (m. 105) **9.** (m. 71)

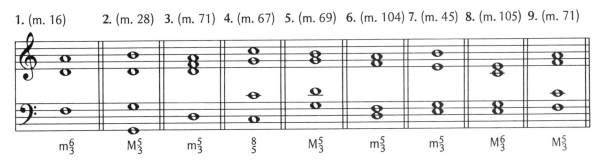

CHORD PROGRESSIONS

At the piano, play the chord progressions given on the bottom two staves while singing the vocalises given on the top staff. If you are not a keyboard player, arpeggiate the progressions on your instrument.

Without the aid of the piano, sing the vocalises and the progressions from the bass up and from the soprano down.

Analyze each progression by numeral as specifically as possible in terms of the tonal center given for it.

1. (mm. 43-44) **2.** (mm. 58-60) **3.** (mm. 72-73)

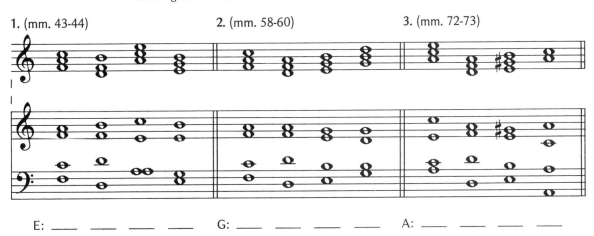

E: ___ ___ ___ ___   G: ___ ___ ___ ___   A: ___ ___ ___ ___

DICTATION AND ANALYSIS

RHYTHM

You will hear one- and two-part excerpts from the work. Notate the *rhythm only* of each excerpt. For each, the number of voice parts, the basic duration, and the suggested number of hearings, respectively, are given in parentheses.

1. (1, ♩, 3)

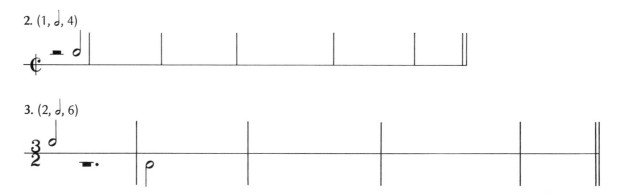

PITCH PATTERNS

Notate in whole notes the nonrhythmicized pitch-pattern excerpts that will be played for you. The suggested number of hearings is given in parentheses.

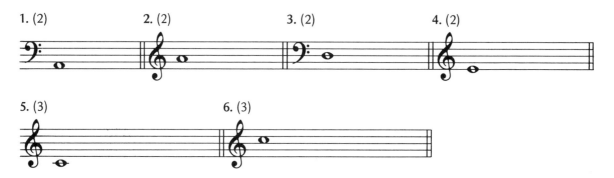

MELODIES

The melodies in this section are presented in two versions: (A) is a *basic* melody—that is, a reduced version of the original melody—and (B) is the *original* melody. Notate the basic melody on staff A and the original melody on staff B. The suggested number of hearings is given in parentheses. (For the original melody, this number is based on your having completed the basic melody first.)

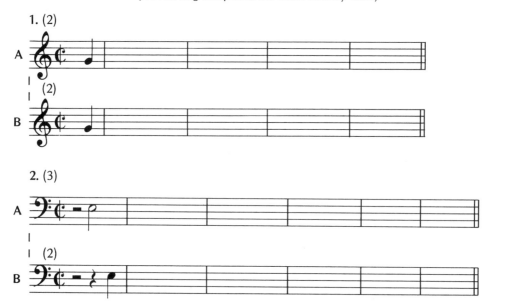

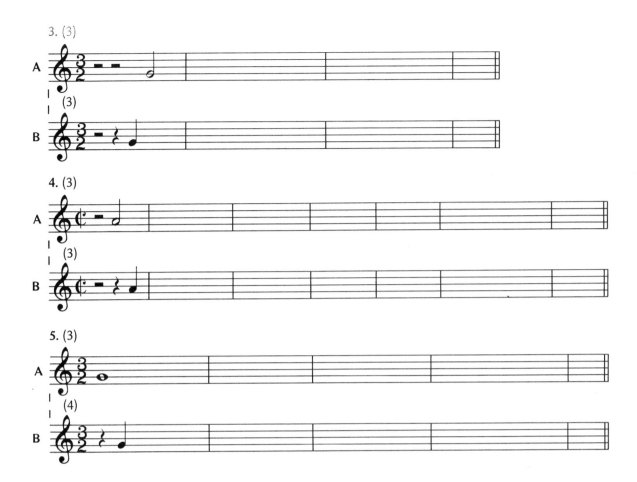

COUNTERPOINT

The exercises in this section are presented in two versions: (A) is a *basic* counterpoint—that is, a reduced version of the original passage—and (B) is the *original* counterpoint. Notate the basic counterpoint on staff A and the original counterpoint on staff B. The suggested number of hearings is given in parentheses. (For the original version, this number is based on your having completed the basic version first.)

3. (4)

SONORITY TYPES

Each of the following items represents a sonority that you are to identify in two hearings. The number of voices in each sonority is given in parentheses.

You are given the highest (stem up) or the lowest (stem down) pitch for each sonority. Notate the other outer voice and as many of the inner voices as you can. Be sure to include any necessary accidentals.

Below each sonority, indicate its sounding chord quality, including inversion (for example, m_4^6, M_3^5, Mm_7, ϕ_5^6).

1. (3)   **2. (3)**   **3. (4)**   **4. (4)**   **5. (4)**   **6. (4)**   **7. (4)**   **8. (4)**

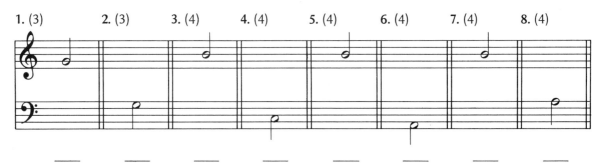

SELECTIVE LISTENING

NONCHORD TONES

In the following exercises you are given the rhythm of the outer voices of excerpts from the work. Each contains nonchord tones, the location of which is indicated by asterisks. From the following list, select the appropriate nonchord tone and place its letter beside the corresponding asterisk. The suggested number of hearings for each exercise is two.

    a. passing tone   d. neighbor tone   g. 4-3 suspension
    b. anticipation   e. 7-6 suspension   h. 2-3 suspension
    c. escape tone   f. 7-6 suspension ornamented

1.

2.

TONAL CHANGE

You will hear three harmonic progressions in which tonal changes occur. For each, the first tonic is given. Add the letter name of the second tonic in each case. The suggested number of hearings for each exercise is two.

1. First tonic: C   second tonic: _____

2. First tonic: C   second tonic: _____

3. First tonic: A   second tonic: _____

PARALLEL INTERVALS

Below you are given the rhythm of the top voice of excerpts from the movement, each of which contains a series of parallel intervals where the brackets appear. From the following list select the appropriate interval and place its letter beside the bracket. The suggested number of hearings is two.

    a. tenths   b. sixths   c. fourths   d. thirds

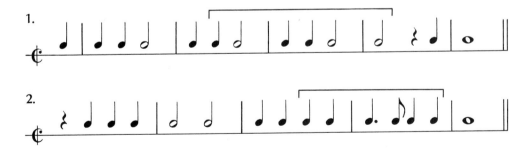

HARMONIC PROGRESSIONS

    The exercises in this section are chordal versions of passages from the work. Notate the outer voices of each progression and add the specific numeral function of each chord that has a blank beneath it. For each chord where an asterisk precedes the blank, you need add only the sonority type. The harmonic rhythm (HR), the first numeral function, the tonal center, and the suggested number of hearings (in parentheses) are given for each exercise.

For the third exercise, two versions are given: (A) is a *basic* version—that is, a reduced version of the original—and (B) is the *original* version. Notate the basic version on staff A and the original version on staff B. (For the original version, the suggested number of hearings is based on your having completed the basic version first.)

1. (3)

C: vi

(HR:

2. (4)

C: iii

(HR:

3. (3)

A

B

A: i

(HR:

CARLO GESUALDO
(c.1560–1613)

Dolcissima mia vita

Dolcissima mia vita is representative of the third and last stage in the development of the sixteenth-century Italian madrigal. It was published in 1611 in Book Five of Gesualdo's seven books of madrigals. Stylistically it occupies a transitional position between the Renaissance and Baroque periods, as evidenced by its treatment of texture. Its meter changes are noteworthy, but its primary appeal lies in Gesualdo's colorful use of harmony, which serves a dramatic purpose, as do his other less spectacular word-painting devices.

Here is a translation of the text:

> My precious love,
> Why do you hesitate to render the assistance I crave?
> Do you perhaps believe that the sweet fire of love which inflames me
> Will be extinguished because you avert your gaze?
> Alas, would that I never had the ardent desire
> To love you or to perish.
>
> (Translation by Donna Cardamone)

GENERAL QUESTIONS

TERMS

Before beginning this unit, make sure you know the meaning of each of the following terms. Check the Glossary at the end of the book for any term that is unfamiliar to you.

RHYTHM	rhythmic density
PITCH	chord mutation, chromatic third relation, cross relation, root movement
TEXTURE	text setting (syllabic, neumatic, melismatic), hocket

GROUP 1

RHYTHM

1. The division of the basic duration is (duple)(triple).

2. The rhythmic density
   a. is consistent throughout   b. alternates between "thin" and "thick"

PITCH

1. This composition
   a. is predominantly diatonic   c. alternates between chromatic
   b. is predominantly chromatic   and diatonic passages

2. The tonal center
   a. does not change   b. changes occasionally   c. changes frequently

3. Important cadences always end on a (major)(minor) chord.

TEXTURE

1. The texture is
   a. quasi-chordal   c. an alternation of quasi-chordal
   b. contrapuntal   and contrapuntal passages

2. How many voices are there?
   a. two   b. three   c. four   d. more than four

FORM

1. Which of the following is the *least* important factor in the work's sectionalization?
   a. change of tonal center   b. change of texture   c. change of harmonic style

2. Throughout the work phrases are generally of (the same)(different) length(s).

GROUP 2

RHYTHM

1. With ♩ as the basic duration, the shortest rhythmic value used is
   a. ♩   b. ♪   c. ♪   d. ♬

2. Phrases begin on
   a. the downbeat   b. the upbeat   c. both (a) and (b)

PITCH

1. The opening sonority is
   a. M_3^5 b. m_3^5 c. m_4^6 d. Mm_7

2. Which of the following nonchord tones is/are most prominently used?
   a. appoggiatura   b. escape tone   c. neighbor tone   d. suspension

TEXTURE   1. This composition is (imitative)(nonimitative).

2. The shortest note value is typically associated with (chordal)(contrapuntal) passages.

FORM   1. (The same)(A different) motive is presented in each contrapuntal passage.

2. Which of the following statements best describes the conclusion of this work?
   a. It concludes with a modified return to the opening material.
   b. It concludes with an exact return to the opening material.
   c. The opening material does not return at the work's conclusion.

GROUP 3

RHYTHM   1. The opening rhythm of the upper voice is

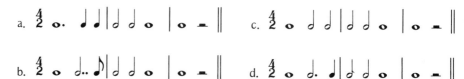

2. The harmonic rhythm of the first phrase is

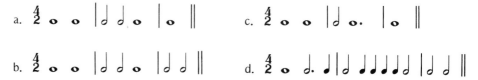

PITCH   1. Which of the following does not/do not appear?
   a. chromatic third-relation   c. cross relation
   b. $\frac{8}{5}$ sonority   d. chord mutation

2. Which of the following patterns represents the opening pitch material of the upper voice?

3. The root movement at the final cadence is
   a. up a major third   c. down a perfect fourth
   b. down a major second   d. down a perfect fifth

TEXTURE   1. Which of the following statements best describes the text setting?
   a. The text setting is syllabic.   c. The text setting is syllabic with
   b. The text setting is neumatic.   melismas on important words.

2. Diatonic writing is associated with (chordal)(contrapuntal) passages.

3. The work contains brief passages in which two parts
   a. are in hocket style   b. move in parallel intervals

FORM   As you listen, write under each lettered bracket in the diagram below the number of the appropriate musical event:

(1) ornamented suspension
(2) imitation
(3) ascending half steps in the soprano
(4) vii°$_6$-I cadence
(5) chords passing over a dominant pedal
(6) repetition of the preceding harmonic progression

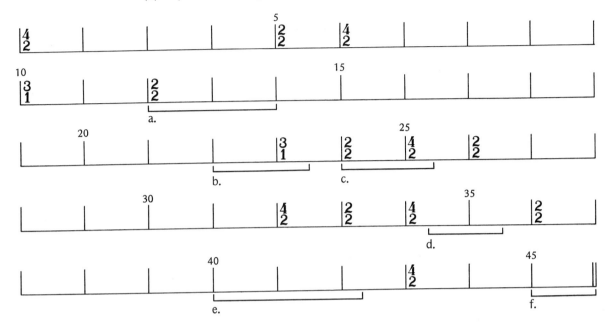

GROUP 4

SCORE STUDY AND DISCUSSION

1. In certain passages—for example, at the opening of the work—the tonal center changes quite often. Determine the various tonics in these instances. How are the changes of tonic brought about? What relationship exists between the last chord of one phrase and the first chord of the next (see, for example, m. 3, m. 8, mm. 10-11)?

2. Examine the motivic organization of contrapuntal passages. Is more than one motive used in each passage? At what intervals are motives imitated? How strict is the imitation?

3. Make a comparative study of this work and the "Gloria" from Josquin's *Missa Pange lingua* (Unit 2). Consider texture, harmonic vocabulary, nonchord tones, and text setting.

PRACTICE DRILLS

RHYTHM

Tap or intone each of the following rhythmic patterns. Then play them on your instrument, being sure to give all notes their full value. (Perform two-line patterns either with another student or at the piano, playing one line while tapping or intoning the other, then reversing the procedure.)

1. (mm. 24-25)

2. (mm. 1-4)

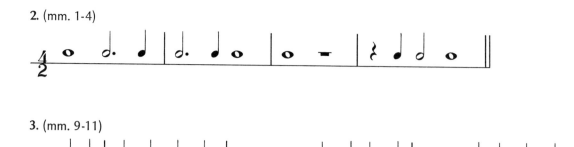

3. (mm. 9-11)

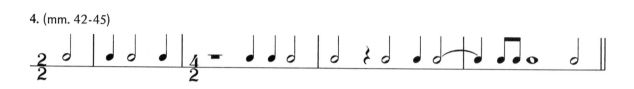

4. (mm. 42-45)

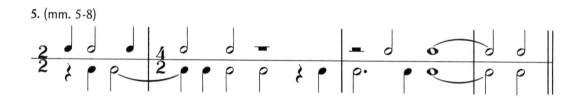

5. (mm. 5-8)

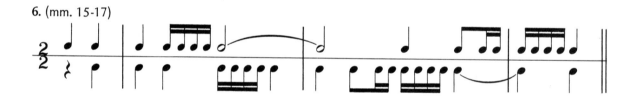

6. (mm. 15-17)

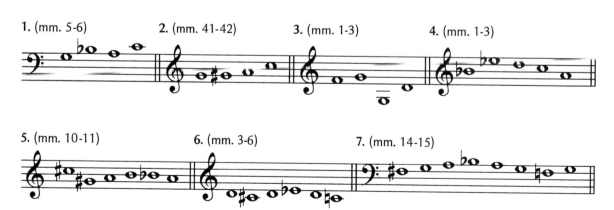

PITCH PATTERNS

Sing each of the following nonrhythmicized pitch-pattern excerpts, transposing up or down an octave as necessary to accommodate your voice range. Then play them on your instrument to check your accuracy.

1. (mm. 5-6)   **2.** (mm. 41-42)   **3.** (mm. 1-3)   **4.** (mm. 1-3)

5. (mm. 10-11)   **6.** (mm. 3-6)   **7.** (mm. 14-15)

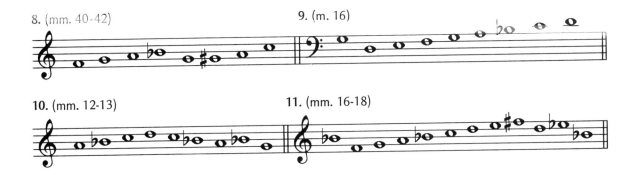

8. (mm. 40-42)   **9.** (m. 16)

10. (mm. 12-13)   **11.** (mm. 16-18)

SONORITY TYPES

Play each of the following sonorities at the piano and sing each tone while the sonority is sounding. Play each sonority again, leaving out one of the tones; sing the missing tone. Repeat this procedure with each of the other tones.

Sing the sonority from the bass up and from the soprano down, using a close spacing to accommodate your voice range.

1. (m. 44)   **2.** (m. 18)   **3.** (m. 21)   **4.** (m. 9)   **5.** (m. 35)   **6.** (m. 35)   **7.** (m. 40)   **8.** (m. 26)   **9.** (m. 4)

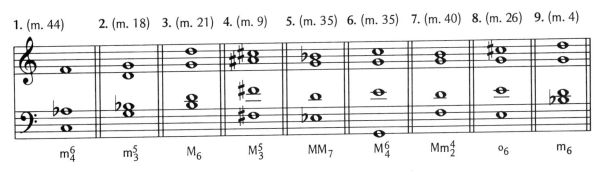

m_4^6 m_3^5 M_6 M_3^5 MM_7 M_4^6 Mm_2^4 $°_6$ m_6

CHORD PROGRESSIONS

At the piano, play the chord progressions given on the bottom two staves while singing the vocalises given on the top staff. If you are not a keyboard player, arpeggiate the progressions on your instrument.

Without the aid of the piano, sing the vocalises and the progressions from the bass up and from the soprano down.

Analyze each progression by numeral as specifically as possible in terms of the tonal center given for it.

1. (mm. 1-2)   **2.** (mm. 2-3)   **3.** (mm. 8-9)   **4.** (m. 11)

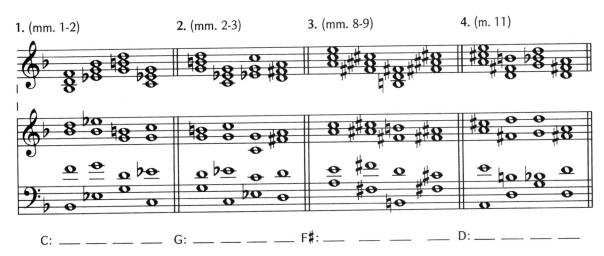

C: __ __ __ __   G: __ __ __ __ __   F#: __ __ __ __ __   D: __ __ __ __

DICTATION AND ANALYSIS

RHYTHM

You will hear one- and two-part excerpts from the work. Notate the *rhythm only* of each excerpt. For each, the number of voice parts, the basic duration, and the suggested number of hearings, respectively, are given in parentheses.

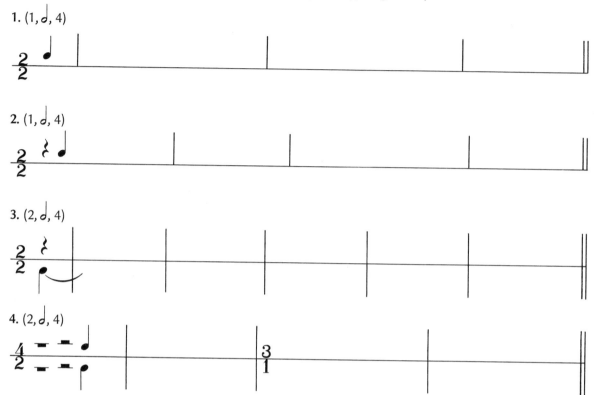

1. (1, ♩, 4)

2. (1, ♩, 4)

3. (2, ♩, 4)

4. (2, ♩, 4)

PITCH PATTERNS

Notate in whole notes the nonrhythmicized pitch-pattern excerpts that will be played for you. The suggested number of hearings is given in parentheses.

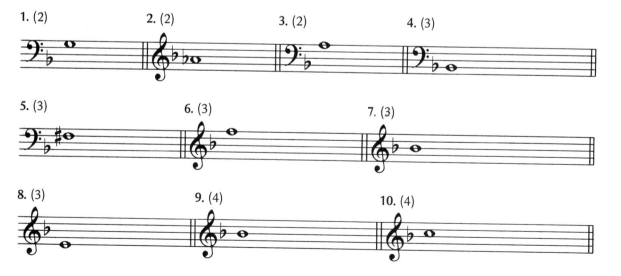

1. (2) 2. (2) 3. (2) 4. (3)

5. (3) 6. (3) 7. (3)

8. (3) 9. (4) 10. (4)

MELODIES

The melodies in this section are presented in two versions: (A) is a *basic* melody—that is, a reduced version of the original melody—and (B) is the *original* melody. Notate the basic melody on staff A and the original melody on staff B. The suggested number of hearings is given in parentheses. (For the original melody, this number is based on your having completed the basic melody first.)

The exercises in this section are presented in two versions: (A) is a *basic* counterpoint—that is, a reduced version of the original passage—and (B) is the *original* counterpoint. Notate the basic counterpoint on staff A and the original counterpoint on staff B. The suggested number of hearings is given in parentheses. (For the original version, this number is based on your having completed the basic version first.)

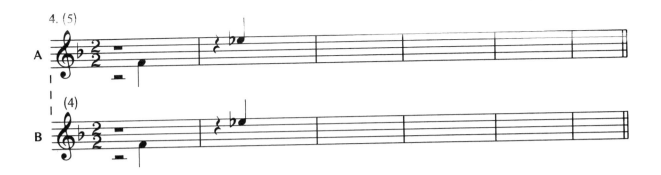

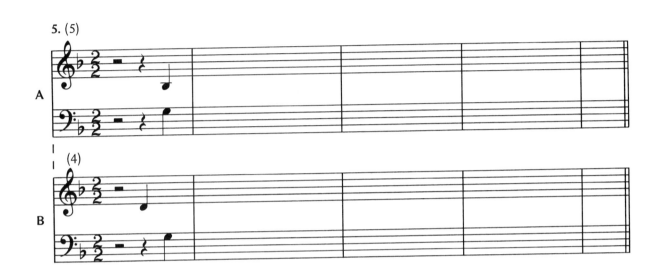

SONORITY TYPES

Each of the following items represents a sonority that you are to identify in two hearings. The number of voices in each sonority is given in parentheses.

You are given the highest (stem up) or the lowest (stem down) pitch for each sonority. Notate the other outer voice and as many of the inner voices as you can. Be sure to include any necessary accidentals.

Below each sonority, indicate its sounding chord quality, including inversion (for example, m^6_4, M^5_3, Mm_7, ϕ^6_5).

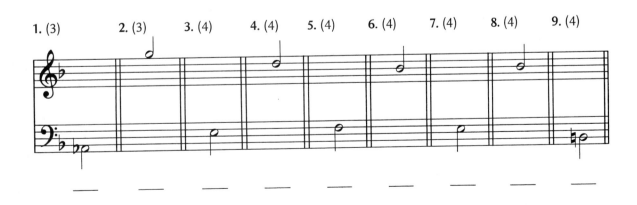

SELECTIVE LISTENING

NONCHORD TONES

In the following exercises you are given the rhythm of two-part excerpts from the work. Each contains nonchord tones, the location of which is indicated by asterisks. From the following list, select the appropriate nonchord tone and place its letter beside the corresponding asterisk. The suggested number of hearings for each exercise is two.

a. 2-3 suspension   d. 9-8 suspension   g. appoggiatura
b. 4-3 suspension   e. passing tone   h. escape tone
c. 7-6 suspension   f. neighbor tone

1.

2.

3.

TONAL CHANGE

You will hear a harmonic progression in which a tonal change occurs. The first tonic is given. Add the letter name of the second tonic and the mode of the first and second key. The suggested number of hearings is two.

1. First tonic: B♭   first mode: _____

2. Second tonic: _____   second mode: _____

PARALLEL INTERVALS

Below you are given the rhythm of the bottom voice of two-part excerpts from the work, each of which contains a series of parallel intervals where the brackets appear. From the following list select the appropriate interval and place its letter beside the bracket. The suggested number of hearings is two.

a. tenths   b. sixths   c. fourths   d. thirds

1.

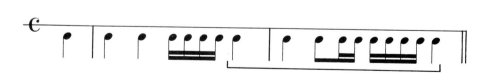

2.

3.

4.

CADENCE TYPES

You will hear an excerpt from the work in which the same cadence is used twice, at points indicated by the brackets in the harmonic rhythm given below. From the following list, select the appropriate cadence. The suggested number of hearings is two.

a. deceptive (V-vi or V-♭VI)
b. authentic (V-I or V-i)
c. plagal (iv-i or IV-I)
d. Phrygian (iv₆-V)

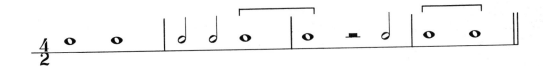

HARMONIC PROGRESSIONS

1. You will hear two excerpts for which the harmonic rhythm is given below. Certain chord progressions have been bracketed. Match each of these progressions to the appropriate item in the list below by placing its letter over the bracket. The suggested number of hearings is given in parentheses.

   a. cadential $^6_4$
   b. chord mutation
   c. plagal cadence
   d. chromatic third relation

a. (2)

b. (3)

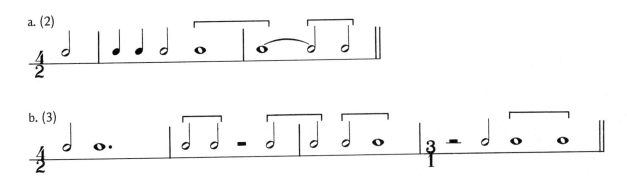

2. The exercises below are chordal versions of passages from the work. Notate the outer voices of each progression and add the specific numeral function of each chord that has a blank beneath it. For each chord where an asterisk precedes the blank, you need add only the sonority type. The harmonic rhythm (HR), the first numeral function, the tonal center, and the suggested number of hearings (in parentheses) are given for each exercise.

a. (2)

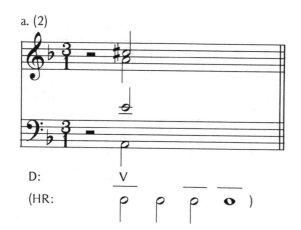

D: V   ___   ___

(HR:

b. (4)

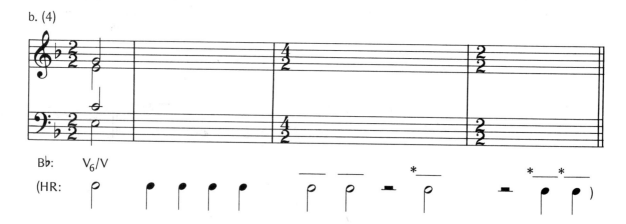

Bb: V$_6$/V

(HR:

HENRY PURCELL
(c.1659–1695)

4

"Oft she visits"
from DIDO AND AENEAS

Purcell's three-act opera *Dido and Aeneas* was composed for a production at a girls' school in Chelsea, England, about 1689. The song "Oft she visits" appears midway through the rather brief second act. The ostinato principle on which the song is based and Purcell's musical portrayal of certain important words in the song are typically Baroque practices.

In the Baroque orchestra, it was traditional for the keyboard player to improvise or "realize" all but the bass line of his part. To guide him, the harmonies of the work were specified in a kind of shorthand by figures appearing under the bass line. At least one other player always doubled the bass line on a gamba, cello, or bassoon. These players constituted the *basso continuo* part (also called *thorough bass* or *figured bass*). Since the figures gave no indication of texture, the keyboard player could realize his part in a variety of ways. The score in this unit gives one possible realization of the continuo part, which will vary from recording to recording, as will the ornamentation of the string parts, where improvisation was also common.

GENERAL QUESTIONS

TERMS

Before beginning this unit, make sure you know the meaning of each of the following terms. Check the Glossary at the end of the book for any term that is unfamiliar to you.

RHYTHM	harmonic rhythm
PITCH	sequence, parallel major, relative major
TEXTURE	text setting (melismatic)
FORM	ground bass, ostinato

GROUP 1

RHYTHM

1. The meter is (simple)(compound).

2. There are (three)(four) basic durations per measure.

3. From time to time the upper line is characterized by (triplets)(dotted rhythms).

PITCH

1. The vocal line begins with an ascending perfect (fourth)(fifth).

2. The widest leap in the first vocal phrase is a
   a. perfect fifth   b. major sixth   c. minor seventh   d. perfect octave

3. The prevailing mode of the work is
   a. major   c. first major, then minor
   b. minor   d. first minor, then major

TEXTURE

Which of the following statements best describes the texture?
   a. All parts are of equal importance.   b. The outer parts dominate the texture.

FORM

1. Into how many main sections does this work fall?
   a. one   b. two   c. three   d. four

2. This work is based on an ostinato figure called a *ground*. Which of the following statements best describes the use of this device?
   a. The ostinato figure is always presented in the upper part.
   b. The ostinato figure is always presented in the lower part.
   c. The ostinato figure migrates from part to part.

GROUP 2

RHYTHM

1. With ♩ as the basic duration, the characteristic rhythmic organization of the ground bass is
   a. alternating eighth and quarter notes
   b. perpetual quarter notes
   c. perpetual eighth notes

2. The number of basic durations in one statement of the ground bass is
   a. eight   b. twelve   c. sixteen

PITCH

1. The mode of the ground bass at the opening of the work is
   - a. harmonic minor
   - b. melodic minor, descending form
   - c. melodic minor, ascending form
   - d. both (b) and (c)

2. Which of the following patterns represents the usual ending of each ground bass statement?

a.　　　　　b.　　　　　c.　　　　　d.

3. The ground bass (does)(does not) contain a sequence.

TEXTURE

Which of the following statements best describes the relationship between the music and the text?
   - a. Textual repetition always coincides with musical repetition.
   - b. Textual repetition never coincides with musical repetition.
   - c. Textual and musical repetition coincide at the opening of the vocal section.
   - d. Textual and musical repetition coincide at the close of the vocal section.

FORM

1. Which of the following statements best describes the relative lengths of the two main sections?
   - a. The ground bass is stated more times in section one than in section two.
   - b. The ground bass is stated more times in section two than in section one.
   - c. The ground bass is stated an equal number of times in sections one and two.

2. Which of the following statements best describes the ground bass?
   - a. Every repetition of the ground bass is the same.
   - b. Every repetition of the ground bass is slightly different.
   - c. Most repetitions of the ground bass are the same, but a few modifications do appear.

GROUP 3

RHYTHM

1. The harmonic rhythm of the opening statement of the ground bass is

   a. $\mathbf{C}$ o | o | 𝅗𝅥 𝅗𝅥 | 𝅗𝅥 𝅗𝅥 ‖

   b. $\mathbf{C}$ 𝅗𝅥 𝅗𝅥 | 𝅗𝅥 𝅗𝅥 | 𝅗𝅥 𝅗𝅥 | 𝅗𝅥 𝅗𝅥 ‖

   c. $\mathbf{C}$ o | o | o | o ‖

   d. $\mathbf{C}$ o | o | 𝅘𝅥 𝅘𝅥 𝅘𝅥 𝅘𝅥 | 𝅗𝅥 𝅗𝅥 ‖

2. (All)(Not all) vocal phrases begin on the downbeat of the measure.

PITCH

1. Phrase repetitions in the melodic line appear at
   - a. the opening of the vocal section
   - b. the close of the vocal section
   - c. the opening of the orchestral section
   - d. the close of the orchestral section

2. In the orchestral section there is a momentary emphasis on the (relative)(parallel) major.

TEXTURE   Among the words depicted musically are "mountain," "in this fountain," and "pursued." Which of the following devices is/are used for word-painting?

a. descriptive melodic contours   c. rapid dotted rhythms
b. changes in orchestral timbre   d. melismas

FORM   Below is a diagram of the thirteen statements of the ground bass. Bracket those areas where a modification of the bass appears. Place a checkmark where there is a cadence on a tonic other than the prevailing one.

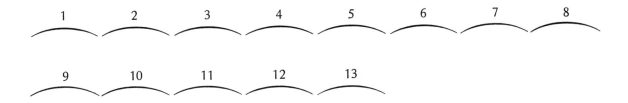

GROUP 4

SCORE
STUDY
AND
DISCUSSION

1. A composer who chooses to write a work based on an ostinato figure faces the problem of counteracting potential monotony. Examine Purcell's treatment of the ground bass. How is it varied and to what effect? How does the phrase structure of the upper line deemphasize the regularity of the ostinato? Explain how the overall form generated by the upper line is also helpful in this regard. Finally, study Purcell's harmonization of each statement of the ground bass. Does it contribute to the solution of this problem?

2. Listen to two or more different performances of this work, concentrating on the continuo part and the ornamentation of the instrumental lines. How do the performances differ from your score?

PRACTICE DRILLS

RHYTHM

Tap or intone each of the following rhythmic patterns. Then play them on your instrument, being sure to give all notes their full value. (Perform two-line patterns either with another student or at the piano, playing one line while tapping or intoning the other, then reversing the procedure.)

1. (mm. 16-18)

2. (mm. 45-49)

3. (mm. 45-49)

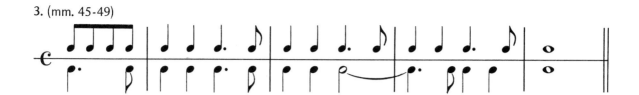

PITCH PATTERNS

Sing each of the following nonrhythmicized pitch-pattern excerpts, transposing up or down an octave as necessary to accommodate your voice range. Then play them on your instrument to check your accuracy.

1. (mm. 45-49)   **2.** (mm. 18-19)

3. (mm. 43-45)   **4.** (mm. 16-18)

SONORITY TYPES

Play each of the following sonorities at the piano and sing each tone while the sonority is sounding. Play each sonority again, leaving out one of the tones; sing the missing tone. Repeat this procedure with each of the other tones.

Sing the sonority from the bass up and from the soprano down, using a close spacing to accommodate your voice range.

1. (m. 27)   **2.** (m. 36)   **3.** (m. 47)   **4.** (m. 34)   **5.** (m. 37)   **6.** (m. 33)

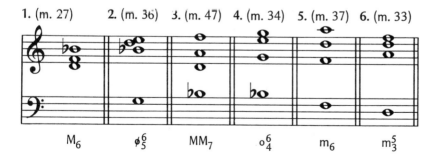

M_6 ϕ^6_5 MM_7 o^6_4 m_6 m^5_3

CHORD PROGRESSIONS

At the piano, play the chord progressions given on the bottom two staves while singing the vocalises given on the top staff. If you are not a keyboard player, arpeggiate the progressions on your instrument.

Without the aid of the piano, sing the vocalises and the progressions from the bass up and from the soprano down.

Analyze each progression as specifically as possible in the key given for it. You may analyze either by chord function class or by numeral.

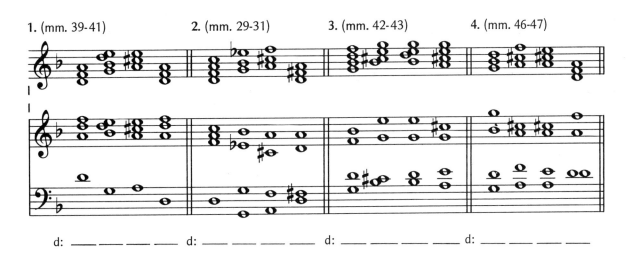

1. (mm. 39-41)   2. (mm. 29-31)   3. (mm. 42-43)   4. (mm. 46-47)

d: _____   d: _____   d: _____   d: _____

DICTATION AND ANALYSIS

RHYTHM

You will hear one-part excerpts from the work. Notate the *rhythm only* of each excerpt. For each, the basic duration and the suggested number of hearings are given in parentheses.

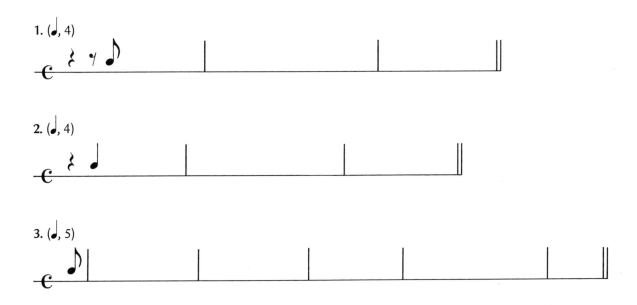

PITCH PATTERNS

Notate in whole notes the nonrhythmicized pitch-pattern excerpts that will be played for you. The suggested number of hearings is given in parentheses.

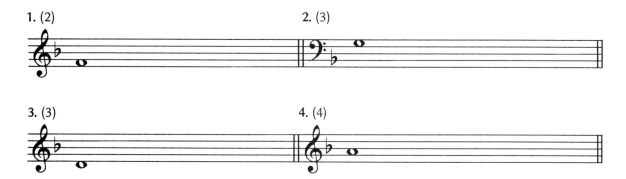

1. (2) **2.** (3)

3. (3) **4.** (4)

MELODIES

The melodies in this section are presented in two versions: (A) is a *basic* melody—that is, a reduced version of the original melody—and (B) is the *original* melody. Notate the basic melody on staff A and the original melody on staff B. The suggested number of hearings is given in parentheses. (For the original melody, this number is based on your having completed the basic melody first.)

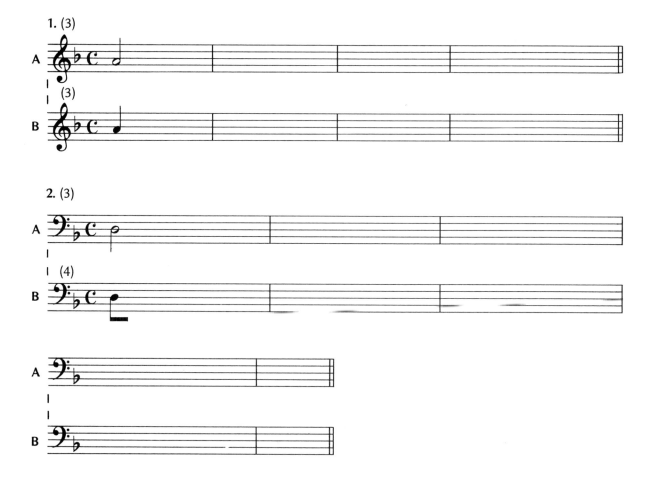

1. (3)

A

(3)

B

2. (3)

A

(4)

B

A

B

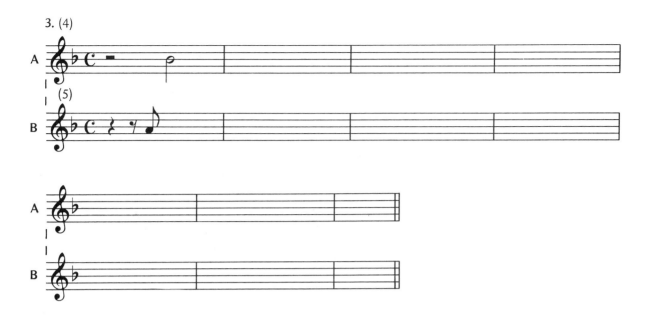

COUNTERPOINT

The exercises in this section are presented in two versions: (A) is a *basic* counterpoint—that is, a reduced version of the original passage—and (B) is the *original* counterpoint. Notate the basic counterpoint on staff A and the original counterpoint on staff B. The suggested number of hearings is given in parentheses. (For the original version, this number is based on your having completed the basic version first.)

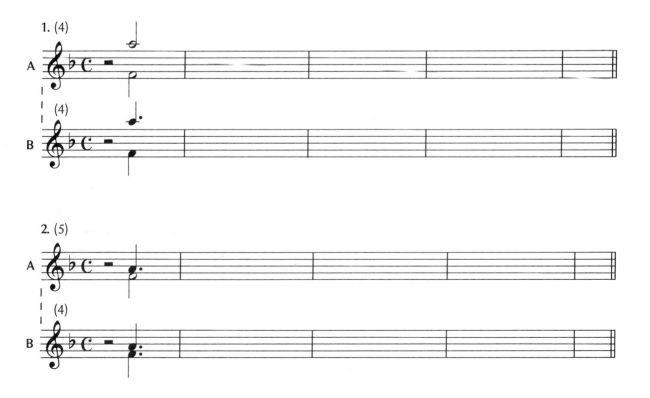

SONORITY TYPES

Each of the following items represents a sonority that you are to identify in two hearings. The number of voices in each sonority is given in parentheses.

You are given the highest (stem up) or the lowest (stem down) pitch for each sonority. Notate the other outer voice and as many of the inner voices as you can. Be sure to include any necessary accidentals.

Below each sonority, indicate its sounding chord quality, including inversion (for example, m$_4^6$, M$_3^5$, Mm$_7$, ø$_5^6$).

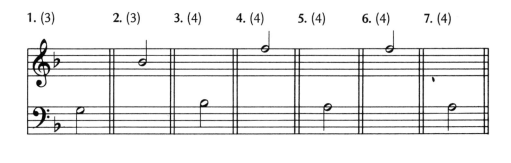

SELECTIVE LISTENING

NONCHORD TONES

In the following exercises you are given the rhythm of the outer voices of excerpts from the work. Each contains nonchord tones, the location of which is indicated by asterisks. From the following list, select the appropriate nonchord tone and place its letter beside the corresponding asterisk. The suggested number of hearings for each exercise is two.

    a. passing tone   c. appoggiatura   e. suspension
    b. neighbor tone   d. escape tone

1.

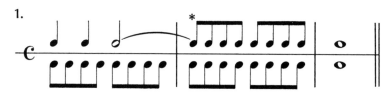

2.

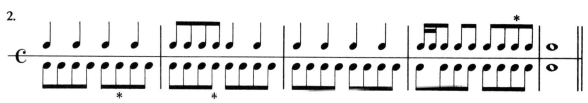

TONAL CHANGE

You will hear a harmonic progression in which a tonal change occurs. The first tonic is given. Add the letter name of the second tonic and the mode of the first and second key. The suggested number of hearings is two.

1. First tonic: D   first mode: ____

2. Second tonic: ____   second mode: ____

The exercises in this section are chordal versions of passages from the work. Notate the outer voices of each progression and add the specific numeral function of each chord that has a blank beneath it. For each chord where an asterisk precedes the blank, you need add only the chord function class. The harmonic rhythm (HR), the first numeral function, the key, and the suggested number of hearings (in parentheses) are given for each exercise.

JOHANN SEBASTIAN BACH
(1685–1750)

Brandenburg Concerto No. 4
THIRD MOVEMENT

This concerto is one of a set of six written in about 1721 during Bach's stay at Cöthen and dedicated to the Margrave Christian Ludwig von Brandenburg, for whose orchestra they were intended.

The term *concerto* as applied to these works is not to be taken in its usual sense, as in the solo concerto of the latter eighteenth and the nineteenth centuries. Rather, the Brandenburg Concertos are examples of "concerted" music in which a soloist or a small solo group (often called the *concertino*) selected from the full orchestra (often called the *tutti* or *ripieno*) performs soloistic passages in alternation with tutti sections. The solo group for this concerto comprises one violin and two flutes (originally, two recorders). As in so much of Bach's music, contrapuntal writing predominates.

Presto

[Solo violin]

[Solo flutes]

Reprinted by permission of Breitkopf & Härtel, Wiesbaden.

GENERAL QUESTIONS

TERMS

Before beginning this unit, make sure you know the meaning of each of the following terms. Check the Glossary at the end of the book for any term that is unfamiliar to you.

RHYTHM	hemiola, syncopation, harmonic rhythm
PITCH	conjunct, disjunct, diatonic, chromatic
TEXTURE	homophony, stretto
FORM	subject, answer

GROUP 1

RHYTHM

1. A plausible metronomic marking for this movement is

    a. ♩ = 50   b. ♩ = 72   c. ♩ = 120

2. The tempo (does) (does not) change within the movement.

3. The number of basic durations per measure is

    a. two   b. three   c. four

PITCH

1. The main melodic materials of the movement are essentially

    a. conjunct and diatonic
    b. disjunct and chromatic
    c. disjunct and diatonic

2. The mode of the movement is

    a. major throughout
    b. major in the first and last sections; both major and minor in interior sections
    c. major for tutti passages; minor for solo passages

TEXTURE

1. The texture throughout the movement is

    a. contrapuntal
    b. mostly contrapuntal, with some homophonic passages
    c. an equal balance of counterpoint and homophony

2. The basic textural plan of the various sections of the movement is

    a. thick at the beginning moving to thinner
    b. thin at the beginning moving to thicker
    c. a combination of (a) and (b)

FORM

Which of the following statements is/are true?

    a. There are three sections of relatively equal length.
    b. The movement is a tonal arch, with the opening and concluding sections in the same tonality, and interior sections in other tonalities.
    c. The movement is sectional, with solo passages helping to set off interior sections.
    d. The movement concludes with a literal return of the materials of the first section.

GROUP 2

RHYTHM

1. Dotted rhythms play a role

   a. during the course of each section
   b. only at main cadences
   c. only in solo sections

2. With 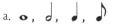 as the basic duration, the range of durations for this movement (not including dotted rhythms) is

PITCH

1. Chordal outlining in melodic passages is prominent in

   a. solo sections (flutes)   b. tutti sections   c. solo sections (violin)

2. Which of the following melodic patterns is characteristic of the bass line at major cadence points?

TEXTURE

Which of the following statements is/are true?

   a. Terraced rather than graded dynamics are characteristic of the movement.
   b. Types of articulation employed in the movement include legato, staccato, and pizzicato.
   c. A registral plan of relatively low tessitura for tutti passages and relatively high tessitura for solo passages helps shape the movement.

FORM

1. Important in delineating the form of the movement are

   a. strong authentic cadences
   b. changes from tutti to solo textures
   c. tonal changes involving distantly related tonalities

2. Which of the following is/are employed during the final portion of the movement?

   a. pedal point   d. harmonic sequence
   b. stretto   e. the full range of durations
   c. the original tonality   in the movement

GROUP 3

RHYTHM

1. Passages featuring the opening melodic subject generally have a harmonic rhythm represented by which of the following?

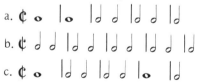

2. Which of the following occur(s) in the movement?

   a. syncopation
   b. a faster harmonic rhythm at major cadence points
   c. hemiola
   d. an effective use of rests (silence) during the concluding portion of the movement

PITCH

1. In measure 5, the opening melodic subject is answered
   a. an octave higher, note for note
   b. at a higher pitch level, with slight intervallic alteration
   c. at a higher pitch level (less than an octave), with no intervallic alteration

2. Which of the following statements is/are true?
   a. During passages in which the tonality is ambiguous, sequences are commonly used to help provide unity.
   b. Phrase structure throughout is regular, with each phrase being four measures long.
   c. Phrases often overlap, with the end of one phrase occurring during the course of, or coinciding with the beginning of, another.

TEXTURE
AND
FORM

Complete the following diagram of the first section of the movement, as begun for you in measures 1-10. *S* means "subject"; *A* means "answer"; the arabic numbers following these letters indicate pitch level from 1 (lowest) to 5 (highest). (The notes at the beginning and end of the diagram are merely for your reference. You need not add the intervening notes.)

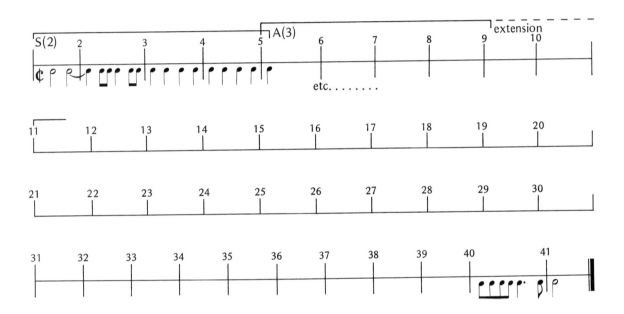

GROUP 4

SCORE
STUDY
AND
DISCUSSION

1. Common to much of Bach's music is more or less continuous motion within sections. Study the score and list as many techniques for achieving this as you can find. For example, in measure 5, the subject ends as the answer begins; and in measure 29 there is a strong cadence in the bass, but the tied notes above cover the cadence. Then listen again to the movement, concentrating on such factors.

2. What techniques (melodic, harmonic, rhythmic, etc.) are used to open the various sections? to bring them to a close? How do these factors contrast with those that produce continuity within sections?

3. Study the score for examples of sequence. Where do sequences appear? Is their purpose primarily to extend passages within a tonality (as in measures 19ff.), or do they serve mainly to effect *changes* in tonality (as in measures 139ff.)? Listen to the movement, concentrating on the sequential passages.

PRACTICE DRILLS

RHYTHM

Tap or intone each of the following rhythmic patterns. Then play them on your instrument, being sure to give all notes their full value. (Perform two-line patterns either with another student or at the piano, playing one line while tapping or intoning the other, then reversing the procedure.)

1. (mm. 1-5)

2. (mm. 1-5)

3. (mm. 61-66)

4. (mm. 189-93)

5. (mm. 25-31)

PITCH PATTERNS

Sing each of the following nonrhythmicized pitch-pattern excerpts, transposing up or down an octave as necessary to accommodate your voice range. Then play them on your instrument to check your accuracy.

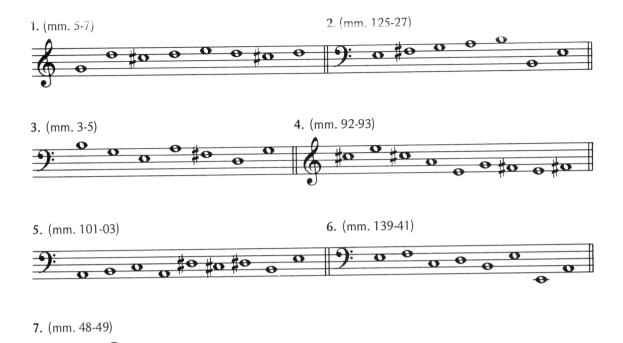

1. (mm. 5-7)   2. (mm. 125-27)

3. (mm. 3-5)   4. (mm. 92-93)

5. (mm. 101-03)   6. (mm. 139-41)

7. (mm. 48-49)

SONORITY TYPES

Play each of the following sonorities at the piano and sing each tone while the sonority is sounding. Play each sonority again, leaving out one of the tones; sing the missing tone. Repeat this procedure with each of the other tones.

Sing the sonority from the bass up and from the soprano down, using a close spacing to accommodate your voice range.

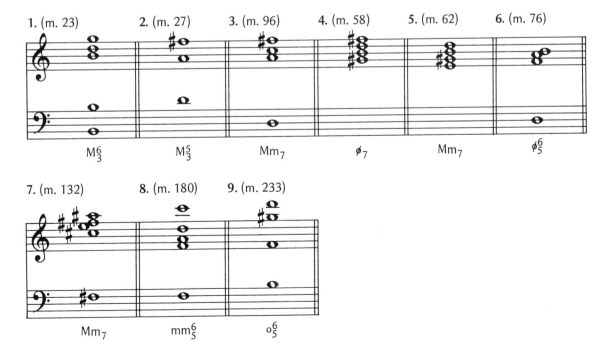

1. (m. 23)   2. (m. 27)   3. (m. 96)   4. (m. 58)   5. (m. 62)   6. (m. 76)

M_3^6 M_3^5 Mm_7 ϕ_7 Mm_7 ϕ_5^6

7. (m. 132)   8. (m. 180)   9. (m. 233)

Mm_7 mm_5^6 o_5^6

CHORD PROGRESSIONS

At the piano, play the chord progressions given on the bottom two staves while singing the vocalises given on the top staff. If you are not a keyboard player, arpeggiate the progressions on your instrument.

Without the aid of the piano, sing the vocalises and the progressions from the bass up and from the soprano down.

Analyze each progression as specifically as possible in the key given for it. You may analyze either by chord function class or by numeral.

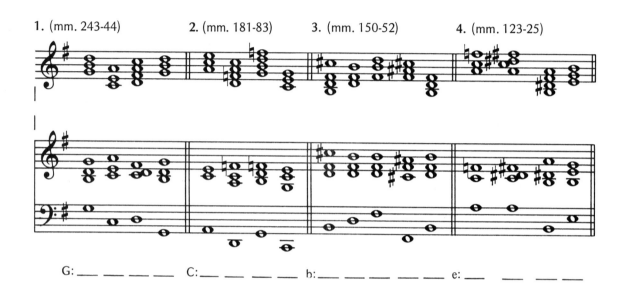

DICTATION AND ANALYSIS

RHYTHM

You will hear one- and two-part excerpts from the work. Notate the *rhythm only* of each excerpt. For each, the number of voice parts, the basic duration, and the suggested number of hearings, respectively, are given in parentheses.

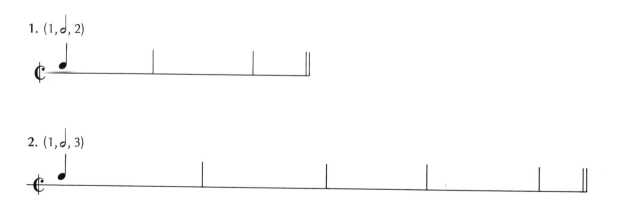

3. (2, ♩, 3)

4. (2, ♩, 3)

5. (2, ♩, 3)

PITCH PATTERNS

Notate in whole notes the nonrhythmicized pitch-pattern excerpts that will be played for you. The suggested number of hearings is given in parentheses.

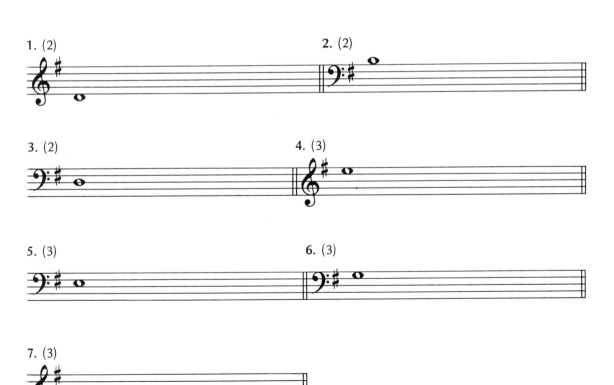

MELODIES

The melodies in this section are presented in two versions: (A) is a *basic* melody—that is, a reduced version of the original melody—and (B) is the *original* melody. Notate the basic melody on staff A and the original melody on staff B. The suggested number of hearings is given in parentheses. (For the original melody, this number is based on your having completed the basic melody first.)

COUNTERPOINT

The exercises in this section are presented in two versions: (A) is a *basic* counterpoint—that is, a reduced version of the original passage—and (B) is the *original* counterpoint. Notate the basic counterpoint on staff A and the original counterpoint on staff B. The suggested number of hearings is given in parentheses. (For the original version, this number is based on your having completed the basic version first.)

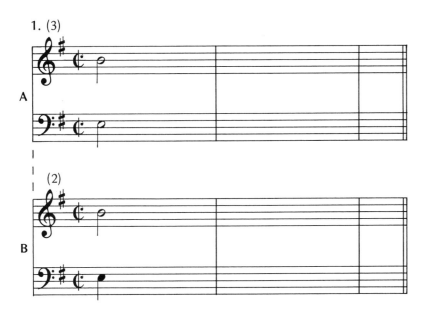

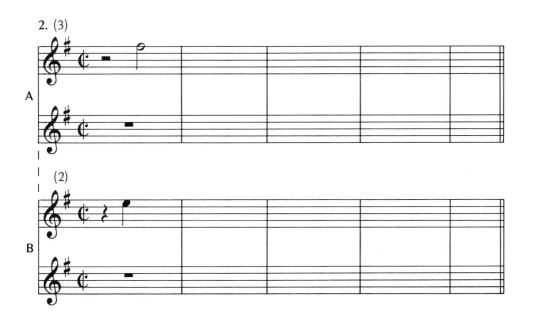

84   BACH: BRANDENBURG CONCERTO NO. 4

SONORITY TYPES

Each of the following items represents a sonority that you are to identify in two hearings. The number of voices in each sonority is given in parentheses.

You are given the highest (stem up) or the lowest (stem down) pitch for each sonority. Notate the other outer voice and as many of the inner voices as you can. Be sure to include any necessary accidentals.

Below each sonority, indicate its sounding chord quality, including inversion (for example, m$_4^6$, M$_3^5$, Mm$_7$, $\emptyset_5^6$).

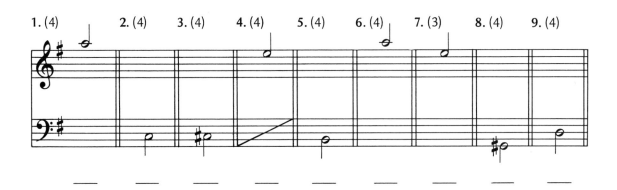

SELECTIVE LISTENING

NONCHORD TONES

In the following exercises you are given the rhythm of the outer voices of excerpts from the work. Each contains nonchord tones, the location of which is indicated by asterisks. From the following list, select the appropriate nonchord tone and place its letter beside the corresponding asterisk. The suggested number of hearings for each exercise is two.

a. passing tone
b. change-of-bass (or change-of-soprano) suspension
c. appoggiatura
d. 4-3 suspension

e. 2-3 suspension
f. escape tone
g. anticipation
h. lower neighbor

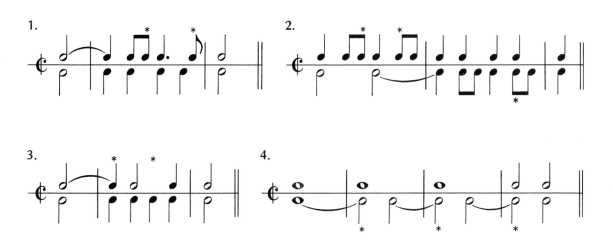

<table>
<tr><td>**TONAL**
CHANGE</td><td>You will hear two harmonic progressions in which tonal changes occur. For each, the first tonic is given. Add the letter name of the second tonic and the mode of the first and second key in each case. The suggested number of hearings for each exercise is two.</td></tr>
</table>

1. First tonic: E   first mode: ____

     Second tonic: ____   second mode: ____

2. First tonic: G   first mode: ____

     Second tonic: ____   second mode: ____

HARMONIC PROGRESSIONS

The exercises in this section are chordal versions of passages from the work. Notate the outer voices of each progression, and the specific numeral function of each chord that has a blank beneath it. The harmonic rhythm (HR), the first numeral function, the key, and the suggested number of hearings (in parentheses) are given for each exercise.

For some of the exercises, two versions are given: (A) is a *basic* version—that is, a reduced version of the original—and (B) is the *original* version. Notate the basic version on staff A and the original version on staff B. (For the original version, the suggested number of hearings is based on your having completed the basic version first.)

1. (3)

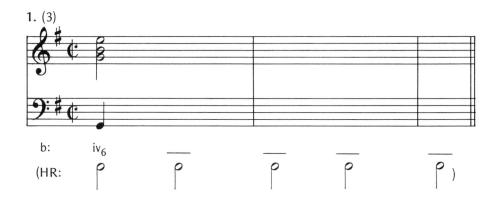

2. (3)

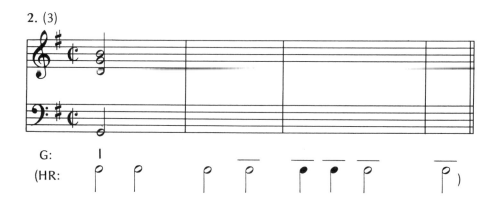

86   BACH: BRANDENBURG CONCERTO NO. 4

3. (3)

4. (3)

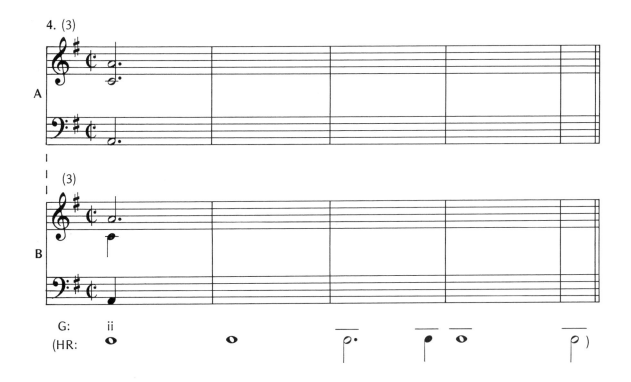

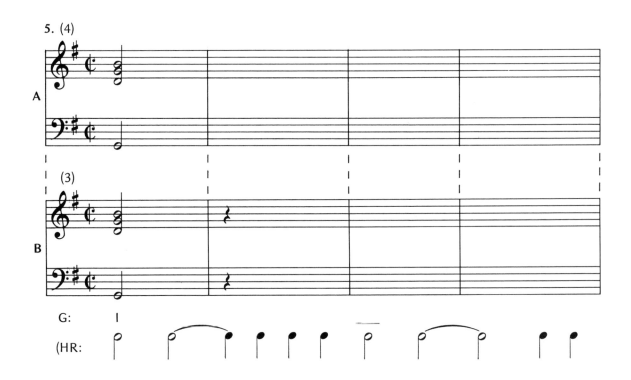

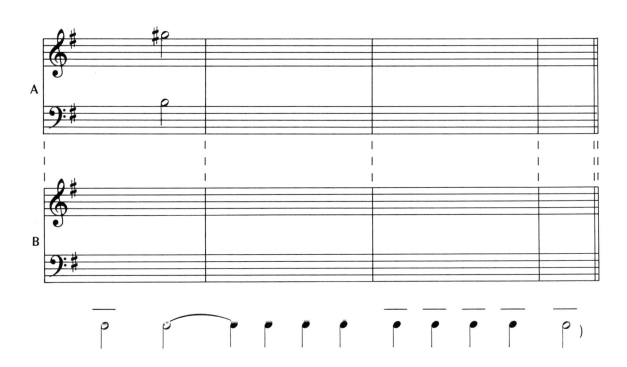

FRANZ JOSEPH HAYDN
(1732–1809)

String Quartet, Op. 74, No. 3
SECOND MOVEMENT

This quartet, sometimes called "The Rider," was written in 1793, the same year in which Haydn composed five other quartets—Op. 71, Nos. 1-3, and Op. 74, Nos. 1 and 2. At that time, Haydn was very much interested in romanticism. An indication of what Haydn's biographer Karl Geiringer calls "the dawn of romanticism" is seen in the key relations of this G minor quartet, the middle movements of which are in the keys of E major and E minor, respectively. Aside from the key relations, other innovative details in this group of quartets include the introductions to the first movements and the emphasis on subsidiary thematic material, a characteristic of later Romantic composers.

The second movement of "The Rider" is simple and straightforward in its overall formal structure and melodic materials. There are few irregularities, although chromaticism does play a role, particularly in the harmonic structure. Notable in the movement is the use of variation as a formal process.

Largo assai

II

Vln. I

Vln. II

Viola

Cello

HAYDN: STRING QUARTET, OP. 74, NO. 3

GENERAL QUESTIONS

TERMS

Before beginning this unit, make sure you know the meaning of each of the following terms. Check the Glossary at the end of the book for any term that is unfamiliar to you.

PITCH   motive, conjunct, disjunct

TEXTURE   homophony, imitation

FORM   variation, return

GROUP 1

RHYTHM

1. Which of the following terms best describes the tempo of the movement?
   a. allegro   b. largo   c. moderato

2. The meter of the movement is
   a. compound duple   b. simple triple   c. simple quadruple

3. The meter (does)(does not) change during the course of the movement.

PITCH

1. Motives (are)(are not) important in the structure of the melodic materials.

2. Melodic materials in the first main section of the movement are primarily
   a. conjunct   b. disjunct   c. a combination of (a) and (b)

3. The first two main sections (are)(are not) in the same mode.

TEXTURE

1. The texture of the movement is primarily
   a. contrapuntal
   b. melody and accompaniment
   c. an even balance between counterpoint and homophony

2. The number of voices is essentially
   a. three   b. four   c. more than four

3. Texture change (is)(is not) important in delineating main sections.

FORM

1. The movement contains (two)(three) main sections.

2. The relationship between the opening and the concluding main sections is best characterized as one of
   a. tonal contrast   b. identity   c. variation

GROUP 2

RHYTHM

1. The rhythm at the opening of the movement is

2. During the course of the movement, the rhythmic activity
   a. increases   b. decreases   c. does not change perceptibly

PITCH　　　　1. Which of the following patterns represents the opening melodic motive?

2. Sonority types common in the movement are

a. triads of all types
b. triads and seventh chords of all types

c. major and minor triads and Mm$_7$ chords

TEXTURE　　　1. Imitation is prominent in the

a. first main section
b. second main section

c. concluding measures of the third main section

2. Register change accompanying the restatement of opening materials occurs in the

a. first main section
b. second main section

c. first and second main sections

3. Which of the following idiomatic string devices occur(s)?

a. double stopping　　b. passage work　　c. tremolo　　d. glissandi

FORM　　　　1. Throughout the movement, phrases are basically

a. two measures long
b. four measures long with a 2 + 2 internal division
c. variable in length

2. Which of the following statements is/are true?

a. The first section has a statement-digression-restatement structure.
b. The second section has two subsections.
c. Both sections conclude with a tonic cadence.
d. The second section is shorter than the first.

GROUP 3

RHYTHM　　　1. Prominent durational relationships of the top voice to the three lower voices are

a. 1:1, 3:1, 4:1　　b. 1:1, 2:1, 4:1　　c. 1:1, 2:1, 3:1

2. Which of the following represent(s) the basic rhythmic motive found in the movement?

a. $\frac{4}{4}$ ♩ ♩♩|♩

b. $\frac{4}{4}$ ♩.. ♫♪.♫♪.♫|♩

c. $\frac{4}{4}$ ♩ ♩ ♪|♩

PITCH　　　　1. On the downbeat of the second, fourth, sixth, eighth, and tenth measures within the first ten measures of the movement, there is a

a. dominant chord　　b. seventh chord　　c. pre-dominant function

2. Within the movement, change of tonal center to other than the original tonic occurs

a. once　　b. twice　　c. more than twice

TEXTURE   Which of the following statements is/are true?

       a. Dynamics and register generally coincide; that is, the higher the pitch, the higher the dynamic level, and vice versa.

       b. The lowest pitch for the first violin part is reached in the second main section.

       c. Both the highest and the lowest pitches in the melody are reached in the concluding section.

FORM   Complete the diagram below of the first main section by 1) adding slurs to group measures into phrases; 2) putting a checkmark over each phrase that begins with the rhythm of the opening motive (or a derivation of it); and 3) adding an asterisk (*) at the point in the second half of the diagram where the opening materials return.

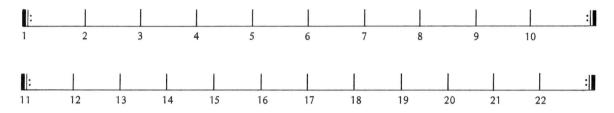

(On some recordings, the repeats may not be made.)

GROUP 4

SCORE
STUDY
AND
DISCUSSION

1. Go through the score without the aid of a piano or recording and mark all cadences. Determine the key in effect at each cadence and the type of cadence (for example, authentic, half). Then listen to the movement while following the score in order to check your analysis. If you missed a key or cadence, study the passage again to determine why.

2. Listen to the movement while following the score. Determine the extent to which the movement as a whole reflects the shape (contour, rhythm, and harmonic structure) of the opening two measures. Can all the materials in the movement be traced back somehow to this opening shape?

PRACTICE DRILLS

RHYTHM

Tap or intone each of the following rhythmic patterns. Then play them on your instrument, being sure to give all notes their full value. (Perform two-line patterns either with another student or at the piano, playing one line while tapping or intoning the other, then reversing the procedure.)

1. (mm. 1-2)

2. (mm. 8-10)

3. (mm. 45-47)

4. (mm. 40-41)

5. (mm. 56-59)

PITCH PATTERNS

Sing each of the following nonrhythmicized pitch-pattern excerpts, transposing up or down an octave as necessary to accommodate your voice range. Then play them on your instrument to check your accuracy.

1. (mm. 1-2)   **2.** (mm. 23-24)   **3.** (mm. 19-22)   **4.** (mm. 19-21)

5. (mm. 11-13)   **6.** (mm. 29-30)   **7.** (mm. 11-14)

SONORITY TYPES

Play each of the following sonorities at the piano and sing each tone while the sonority is sounding. Play each sonority again, leaving out one of the tones; sing the missing tone. Repeat this procedure with each of the other tones.

Sing the sonority from the bass up and from the soprano down, using a close spacing to accommodate your voice range.

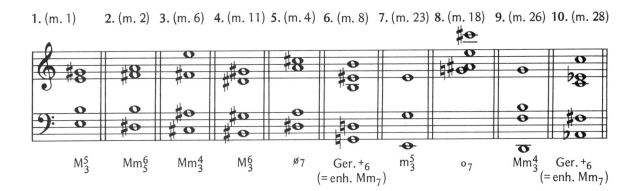

1. (m. 1) 2. (m. 2) 3. (m. 6) 4. (m. 11) 5. (m. 4) 6. (m. 8) 7. (m. 23) 8. (m. 18) 9. (m. 26) 10. (m. 28)

M_3^5 Mm_5^6 Mm_3^4 M_3^6 $\emptyset 7$ Ger. $^+6$ m_3^5 $^o7$ Mm_3^4 Ger. $^+6$
(= enh. Mm_7) (= enh. Mm_7)

CHORD PROGRESSIONS

At the piano, play the chord progressions given on the bottom two staves while singing the vocalises given on the top staff. If you are not a keyboard player, arpeggiate the progressions on your instrument.

Without the aid of the piano, sing the vocalises and the progressions from the bass up and from the soprano down, using a close spacing to accommodate your voice range.

Analyze each progression as specifically as possible in the key given for it. You may analyze either by chord function class or by numeral.

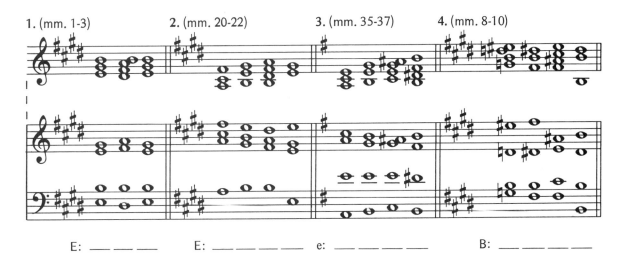

1. (mm. 1-3)   2. (mm. 20-22)   3. (mm. 35-37)   4. (mm. 8-10)

E: ___ ___ ___   E: ___ ___ ___ ___   e: ___ ___ ___ ___   B: ___ ___ ___ ___

DICTATION AND ANALYSIS

RHYTHM

You will hear one- and two-part excerpts from the work. Notate the *rhythm only* of each excerpt. For each, the number of voice parts, the basic duration, and the suggested number of hearings, respectively, are given in parentheses.

1. (1, ♩, 3)

2. (1, ♩, 3)

3. (1, ♩, 3)

4. (2, ♩, 3)

5. (2, ♩, 3)

PITCH PATTERNS

Notate in whole notes the nonrhythmicized pitch-pattern excerpts that will be played for you. The suggested number of hearings is given in parentheses.

1. (2)   **2.** (2)   **3.** (2)

4. (3)   **5.** (3)

6. (3)

MELODIES

The melodies in this section are presented in two versions: (A) is a *basic* melody—that is, a reduced version of the original melody—and (B) is the *original* melody. Notate the basic melody on staff A and the original melody on staff B. The suggested number of hearings is given in parentheses. (For the original melody, this number is based on your having completed the basic melody first.)

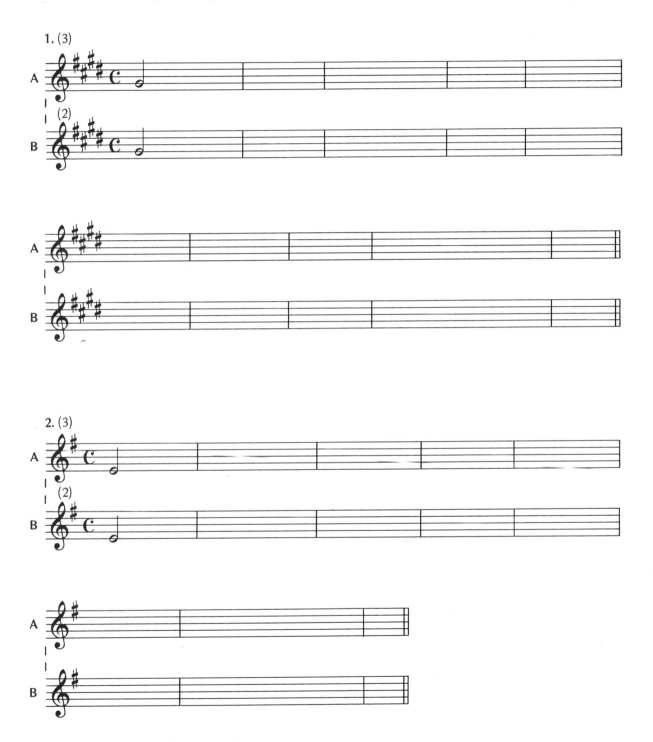

SONORITY TYPES

Each of the following items represents a sonority that you are to identify in two hearings. The number of voices in each sonority is given in parentheses.

You are given the highest (stem up) or the lowest (stem down) pitch for each sonority. Notate the other outer voice and as many of the inner voices as you can. Be sure to include any necessary accidentals.

Below each sonority, indicate its sounding chord quality, including inversion (for example, m_3^5, M_4^6, Mm_7, ϕ_5^6).

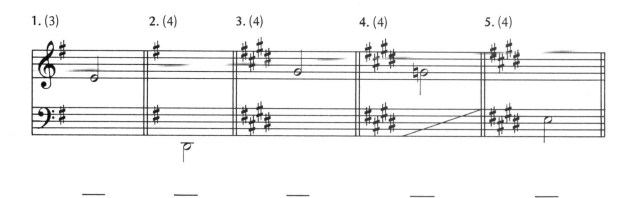

SELECTIVE LISTENING

NONCHORD TONES

In the following exercises you are given the rhythm of the outer voices of two excerpts from the movement. Each contains nonchord tones, the location of which is indicated by asterisks. From the following list, select the appropriate nonchord tone and place its letter beside the corresponding asterisk. The suggested number of hearings for each exercise is two.

    a. neighbor tone   c. passing tone   e. suspension
    b. escape tone   d. appoggiatura

1.

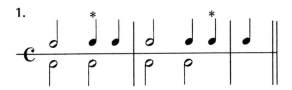

2.

TONAL CHANGE

You will hear two harmonic progressions in which tonal changes occur. For each, the first tonic is given. Add the letter name of the second tonic and the mode of the first and second key in each case. The suggested number of hearings for each exercise is two.

1. First tonic: E   first mode: ____
   Second tonic: ____   second mode: ____

2. †First tonic: C   first mode: ____
   Second tonic: ____   second mode: ____

†You will hear a C major triad to help orient you; the example does not begin on I.

HARMONIC PROGRESSIONS

The exercises in this section are chordal versions of passages from the movement. Notate the outer voices of each progression and add the specific numeral function of each chord that has a blank beneath it. For each chord where an asterisk precedes the blank, you need add only the chord function class. The harmonic rhythm (HR), the first numeral function, the key, and the suggested number of hearings (in parentheses) are given for each exercise.

For the fourth exercise, two versions are given: (A) is a *basic* version—that is, a reduced version of the original—and (B) is the *original* version. Notate the basic version on staff A and the original version on staff B. (For the original version, the suggested number of hearings is based on your having completed the basic version first.)

1. (3)

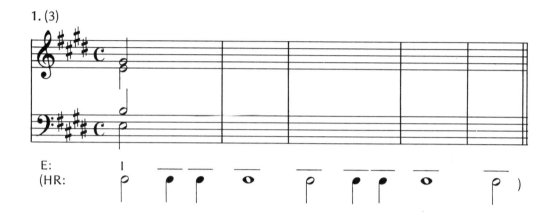

2. (3)

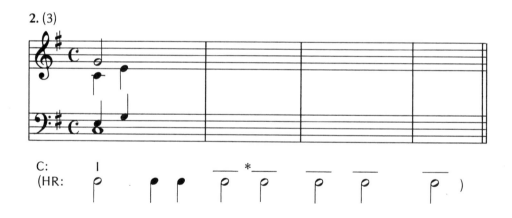

3. (3)

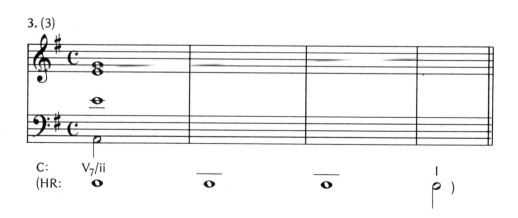

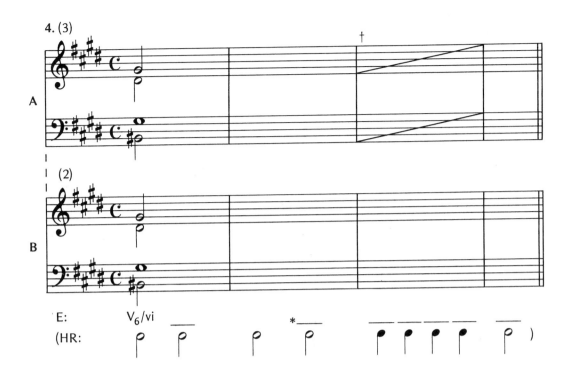

4. (3)

A

(2)

B

E: V$_6$/vi

(HR:

†The third measure of the original version contains chords that embellish the second chord of measure 2 and its motion to the first chord of measure 4. As such, the contents of that measure do not affect the basic progression.

WOLFGANG AMADEUS MOZART
(1756–1791)

String Quintet, K. 516
FIRST MOVEMENT

The G minor Quintet, for two violins, two violas, and cello, was composed along with three other quintets (K. 515, K. 593, and K. 614) during the years 1787-91. There is reason to think that Mozart intended to dedicate these quintets to the new king of Prussia as soon as he had completed two more to make a group of six. But because of his desperate need for money, Mozart was forced to allow two of the quintets (K. 515 and K. 516) and a quintet transcription (K. 406) to be published on a subscription basis.

In the first movement of K. 516, we see Mozart's concern with giving interesting parts to the other instruments as well as to the first violin, which had traditionally enjoyed the greatest share of the activity in string chamber works. Notable in this movement are chromaticism, an interesting twist in the tonality of the second theme, and fluent counterpoint.

*) Zu einer ursprünglichen Fassung der Takte 72 und 74 in Violine I bzw. der Takte 73 und 75 im Violoncello vgl. Krit. Bericht.

*) Zu einer ursprünglichen Fassung der Takte 209 und 211 in Violine I bzw. der Takte 210 und 212 im Violoncello vgl. Krit. Bericht.

GENERAL QUESTIONS

TERMS

Before beginning this unit, make sure you know the meaning of each of the following terms. Check the Glossary at the end of the book for any term that is unfamiliar to you.

RHYTHM	diminution, syncopation
PITCH	conjunct, disjunct, chromatic, sequence, inversion, imitation, ninth chords
TEXTURE	homophony
FORM	sonata form

GROUP 1

RHYTHM

1. Which of the following terms best describes the tempo of the movement?

   a. presto   b. allegro   c. moderato

2. The primary division of the basic duration is (simple)(compound).

3. The meter (does)(does not) change during the course of the movement.

PITCH

1. The first chord function of the movement is (tonic)(dominant).

2. The first pitch heard is a D. The tonal center of the opening section is

   a. B♭ major   b. E♭ major   c. G minor   d. D minor

3. The primary melodic materials are essentially (conjunct)(disjunct).

4. Motives (are)(are not) important in the structure of the themes.

TEXTURE

1. The texture of the movement is

   a. contrapuntal
   b. melody and accompaniment
   c. primarily melody and accompaniment but with considerable contrapuntal activity

2. Texture tends to be thicker toward the (beginning)(middle)(end) of each main section.

FORM

1. The movement consists of

   a. two main sections plus a coda
   b. three main sections plus a coda
   c. four main sections plus a coda

2. Which of the following main sections are most closely related structurally?

   a. first and second   b. second and third   c. first and third

GROUP 2

RHYTHM

1. During the course of the movement, the basic duration (♩ in a fast tempo) is subdivided into which of the following patterns?

   a.   b.   c.   d.

2. Which of the following help(s) to bring about a conclusion to the first and third main sections of the movement?

    a. progressive diminution of note values from ♩♩ to ♩♩♩ (³) to ♪♪♪♪

    b. syncopation

    c. increasingly complex rhythmic texture within each section

PITCH

1. Chromaticism in the movement is prominent in

    a. the initial presentation of each of the main themes

    b. sequential materials leading to major cadences

    c. the second main section

2. The second theme in the first main section begins in

    a. tonic and moves to ♭III

    b. tonic and moves to V

    c. ♭III and moves to V

TEXTURE

1. The cello

    a. is solely a bass-line player

    b. participates equally with the other instruments in presenting melodic material

    c. is essentially a bass-line player but also helps present some melodic material

2. Contrapuntal activity within the movement

    a. consists of, at most, two separate voices with accompaniment

    b. at times involves as many as four separate voices presenting different melodic materials

    c. is confined to the second main formal section

FORM

1. Which of the following play(s) an important role in delineating form in this movement?

    a. tonal change   b. textural change   c. cadences   d. (a), (b), and (c)

2. The first main section consists of how many subsections?

    a. two   b. three   c. four

GROUP 3

RHYTHM

Harmonic rhythm in the movement

    a. is consistently two root changes per measure

    b. is generally faster in the first theme than in the second

    c. always involves two root changes in the measure prior to a major cadence

PITCH

1. Which of the following statements describe(s) the relationship between the first and second main themes?

    a. Both include skips stressing tonic chord members.

    b. Both begin with anacruses (pickups).

    c. Both remain within the tonic key.

    d. Both have initial four-measure phrases.

2. Which of the following cadence types is/are prominent in the movement?

    a. half   b. deceptive   c. authentic

3. Which of the following techniques appear(s)?

    a. sequence   b. imitation   c. melodic inversion   d. (a), (b), and (c)

TEXTURE	1. Change of register to restate thematic materials occurs prominently

TEXTURE

1. Change of register to restate thematic materials occurs prominently
    a. in the opening section within the exposition of the first theme
    b. in the opening section within the exposition of the second theme
    c. at the beginning of the third main section (as compared with the beginning of the movement)

2. Which of the following play(s) a major role in the presentation of thematic materials?
    a. staccato and legato articulation
    b. double stops
    c. changing tessitura within each theme section

FORM

1. The second main section of the movement
    a. introduces new melodic materials
    b. provides tonal instability
    c. presents fragmented thematic materials
    d. concludes with a dominant pedal point

2. In which of the following ways is the second main section like the first?
    a. The order of presentation of thematic materials is the same.
    b. The subsections are clearly separated by cadences.
    c. The tonality at the end of the section is different from that at the beginning.

GROUP 4

SCORE
STUDY
AND
DISCUSSION

1. The structural design represented by this movement is *sonata-allegro* (or simply *sonata*) form.
    a. Study the exposition and recapitulation sections carefully for their materials. How are the two sections alike? How are they different? What reasons can you suggest for the differences between the two sections?
    b. Study the development section. Does it fall into subsections? What previous materials appear? How are they used? What role does this section of the movement fulfill?
    Now listen again to the movement while following the score and concentrating on the three sections and their internal structure.

2. The opening theme of the movement establishes a pattern of phrases that are four measures long. However, our expectation that this pattern will continue is thwarted many times by a change in phrase length. Study the score of the movement and note all instances of other than four-measure phrases. Where do these variations in phrase length appear? What purpose do they serve? Listen again to the movement, concentrating on the phrase structure.

PRACTICE DRILLS

RHYTHM

Tap or intone each of the following rhythmic patterns. Then play them on your instrument, being sure to give all notes their full value. (Perform two-line patterns either with another student or at the piano, playing one line while tapping or intoning the other, then reversing the procedure.)

1. (mm. 34-39)

2. (mm. 43-46)

3. (mm. 68-72)

4. (mm. 118-22)

PITCH PATTERNS

Sing each of the following nonrhythmicized pitch-pattern excerpts, transposing up or down an octave as necessary to accommodate your voice range. Then play them on your instrument to check your accuracy.

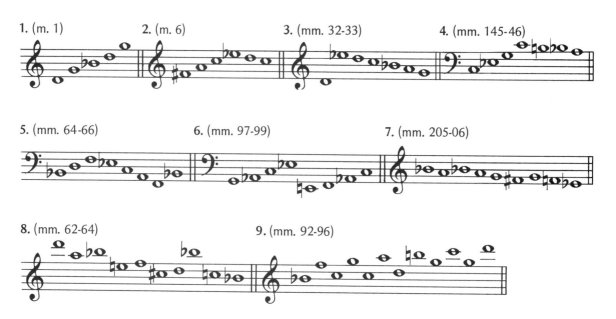

1. (m. 1) **2.** (m. 6) **3.** (mm. 32-33) **4.** (mm. 145-46)

5. (mm. 64-66) **6.** (mm. 97-99) **7.** (mm. 205-06)

8. (mm. 62-64) **9.** (mm. 92-96)

SONORITY TYPES

Play each of the following sonorities at the piano and sing each tone while the sonority is sounding. Play each sonority again, leaving out one of the tones; sing the missing tone. Repeat this procedure with each of the other tones.

Sing the sonority from the bass up and from the soprano down, using a close spacing to accommodate your voice range.

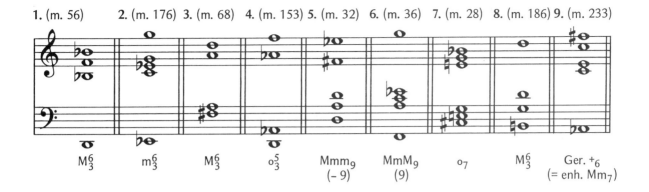

CHORD PROGRESSIONS

At the piano, play the chord progressions given on the bottom two staves while singing the vocalises given on the top staff. If you are not a keyboard player, arpeggiate the progressions on your instrument.

Without the aid of the piano, sing the vocalises and the progressions from the bass up and from the soprano down, using a close spacing to accommodate your voice range.

Analyze each progression as specifically as possible in the key given for it. You may analyze either by chord function class or by numeral.

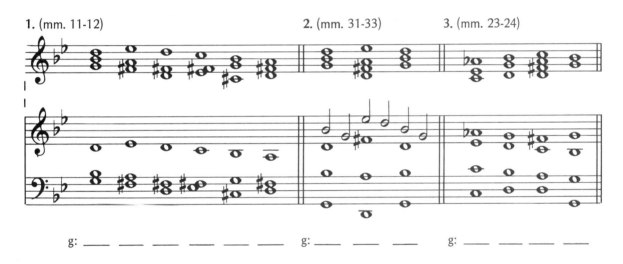

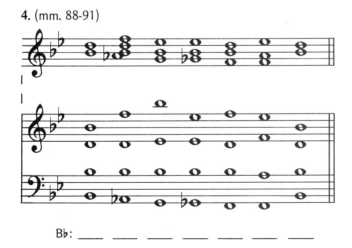

DICTATION AND ANALYSIS

RHYTHM

You will hear one- and two-part excerpts from the work. Notate the *rhythm only* of each excerpt. For each, the number of voice parts, the basic duration, and the suggested number of hearings, respectively, are given in parentheses.

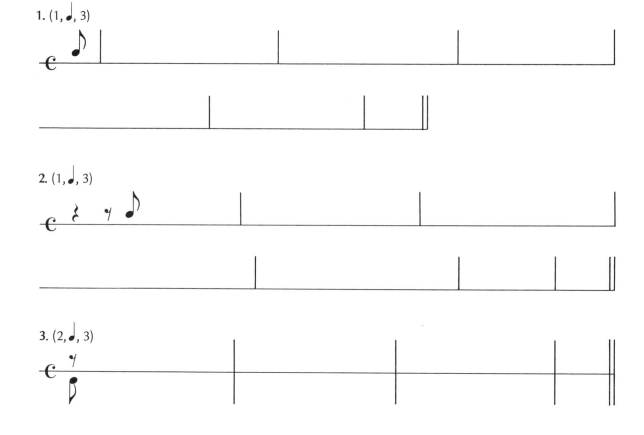

1. (1, ♩, 3)

2. (1, ♩, 3)

3. (2, ♩, 3)

4. (2, ♩, 4)

PITCH PATTERNS

Notate in whole notes the nonrhythmicized pitch-pattern excerpts that will be played for you. The suggested number of hearings is given in parentheses.

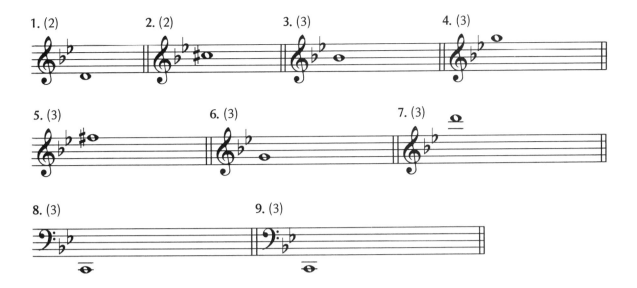

MELODIES

The melodies in this section are presented in two versions: (A) is a *basic* melody—that is, a reduced version of the original melody—and (B) is the *original* melody. Notate the basic melody on staff A and the original melody on staff B. The suggested number of hearings is given in parentheses. (For the original melody, this number is based on your having completed the basic melody first.)

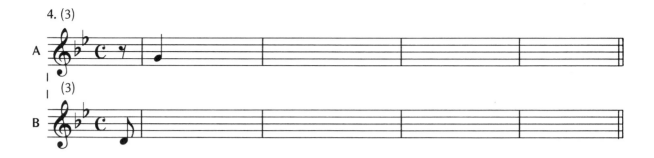

4. (3)

A

(3)

B

COUNTERPOINT

The exercises in this section are presented in two versions: (A) is a *basic* counterpoint—that is, a reduced version of the original passage—and (B) is the *original* counterpoint. Notate the basic counterpoint on staff A and the original counterpoint on staff B. The suggested number of hearings is given in parentheses. (For the original version, this number is based on your having completed the basic version first.)

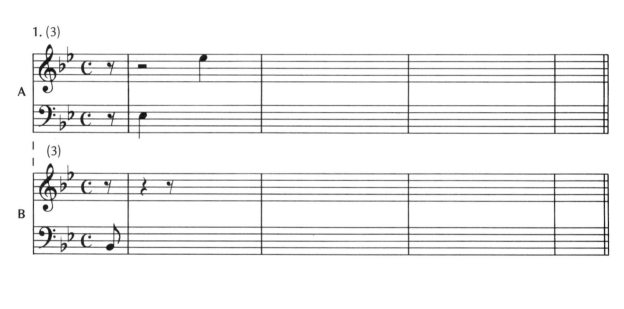

1. (3)

A

(3)

B

2. (3)

A

(3)

B

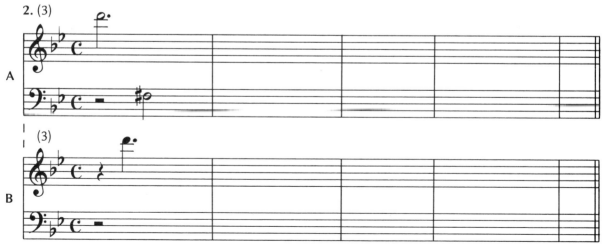

3. (4)

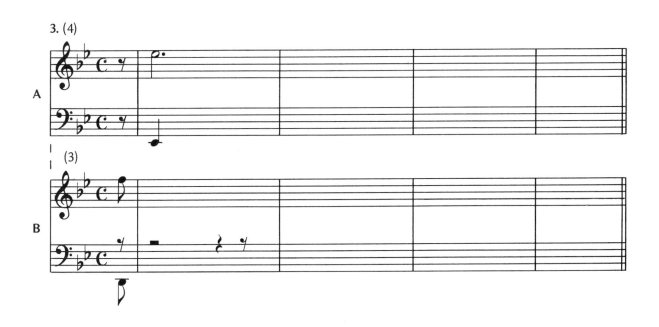

(3)

4. (4)

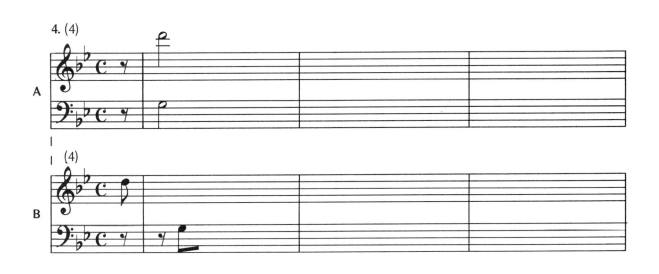

(4)

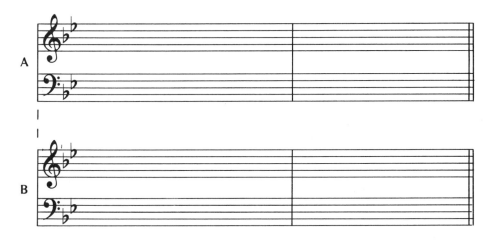

5. (4)

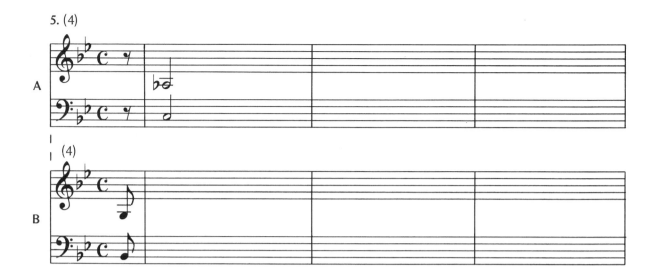

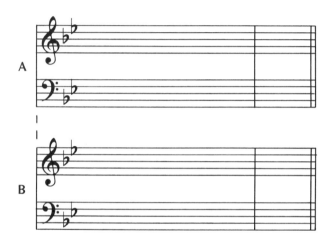

SONORITY TYPES

Each of the following items represents a sonority that you are to identify in two hearings. The number of voices in each sonority is given in parentheses.

You are given the highest (stem up) or the lowest (stem down) pitch for each sonority. Notate the other outer voice and as many of the inner voices as you can. Be sure to include any necessary accidentals.

Below each sonority, indicate its sounding chord quality, including inversion (for example, m_3^5, M_4^6, Mm_7, ϕ_5^6).

1. (6)   **2. (6)**   **3. (4)**   **4. (5)**   **5. (6)**   **6. (6)**   **7. (5)**   **8. (6)**   **9. (4)**

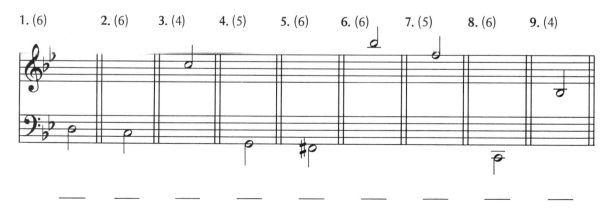

SELECTIVE LISTENING

NONCHORD TONES

In the following exercises you are given the rhythm of the outer voices of excerpts from the work. Each contains nonchord tones, the location of which is indicated by asterisks. From the following list, select the appropriate nonchord tone and place its letter beside the corresponding asterisk. The suggested number of hearings for each exercise is two.

a. suspension   c. appoggiatura   e. anticipation
b. escape tone   d. neighbor tone   f. passing tone

1.

2.

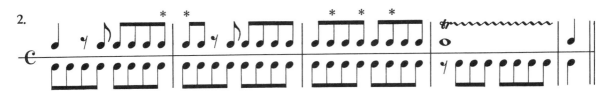

TONAL CHANGE

You will hear three harmonic progressions in which tonal changes occur. For each, the first tonic is given. Add the letter name of the second tonic and the mode of the first and second key in each case. The suggested number of hearings for the first two progressions is two; for the third, three.

1. First tonic: G   first mode: ____
   Second tonic: ____   second mode: ____

2. First tonic: G   first mode: ____
   Second tonic: ____   second mode: ____

3. First tonic: D♭   first mode: ____
   Second tonic: ____   second mode: ____

HARMONIC FUNCTION

Below you are given the rhythm of the outer voices of two chordal excerpts from the movement. Add the specific numeral function of each chord that has a blank beneath it. Where an asterisk precedes the blank, you need add only the chord function class. The suggested number of hearings for each excerpt is three.

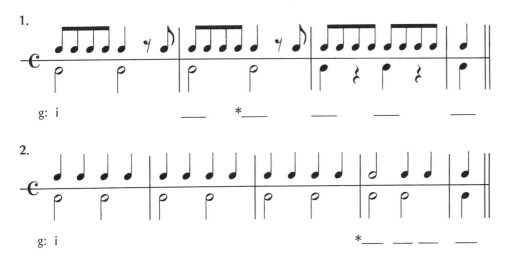

HARMONIC PROGRESSIONS

The exercises in this section are chordal versions of passages from the movement. Notate the outer voices of each progression, and add the specific numeral function of each chord that has a blank beneath it. For each chord where an asterisk precedes the blank, you need add only the chord function class. The harmonic rhythm (HR), the first numeral function, the key, and the suggested number of hearings (in parentheses) are given for each exercise.

For some of the exercises, two versions are given: (A) is a *basic* version—that is, a reduced version of the original—and (B) is the *original* version. Notate the basic version on staff A and the original version on staff B. (For the original version, the suggested number of hearings is based on your having completed the basic version first.)

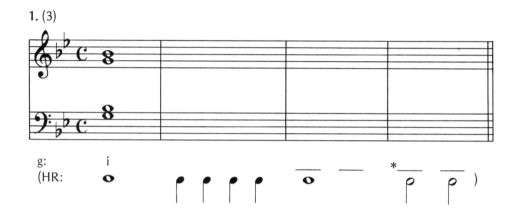

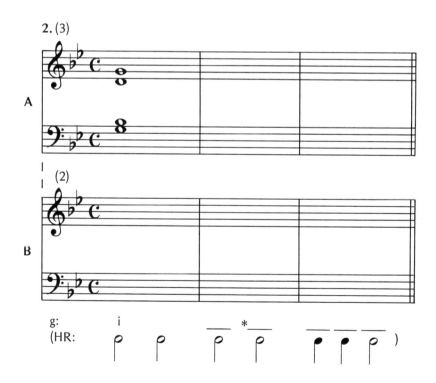

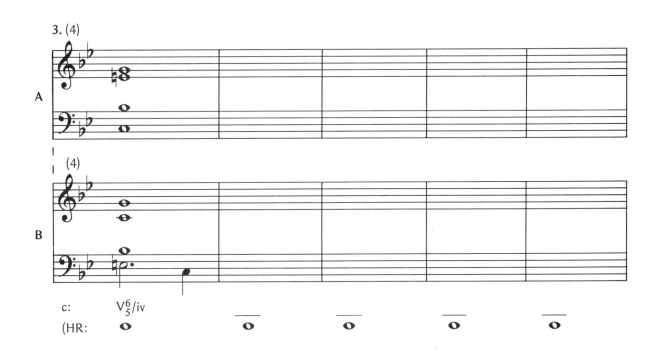

3. (4)

A

(4)

B

c: V⁶₅/iv

(HR:

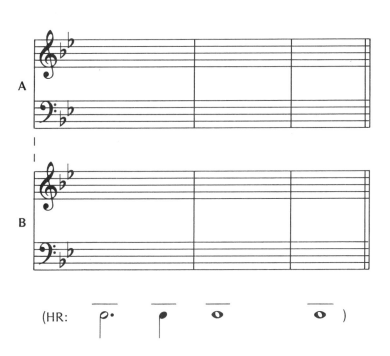

A

B

(HR:)

LUDWIG VAN BEETHOVEN
(1770–1827)

Symphony No. 7, Op. 92
SECOND MOVEMENT

The Seventh Symphony was first performed in Vienna in 1813 with Beethoven conducting. The second movement combines the *variation* and *rondo* principles by interpolating three episodes (the second quite brief) into a theme and seven variations. Particularly interesting in the theme and first three variations is the coordination of dynamics, texture, and orchestration to create a single formal unit. Other notable aspects of this movement are the use of one of the variations as a development section and the exploitation of orchestral timbres in another.

Reprinted by permission of Breitkopf & Härtel, Wiesbaden.

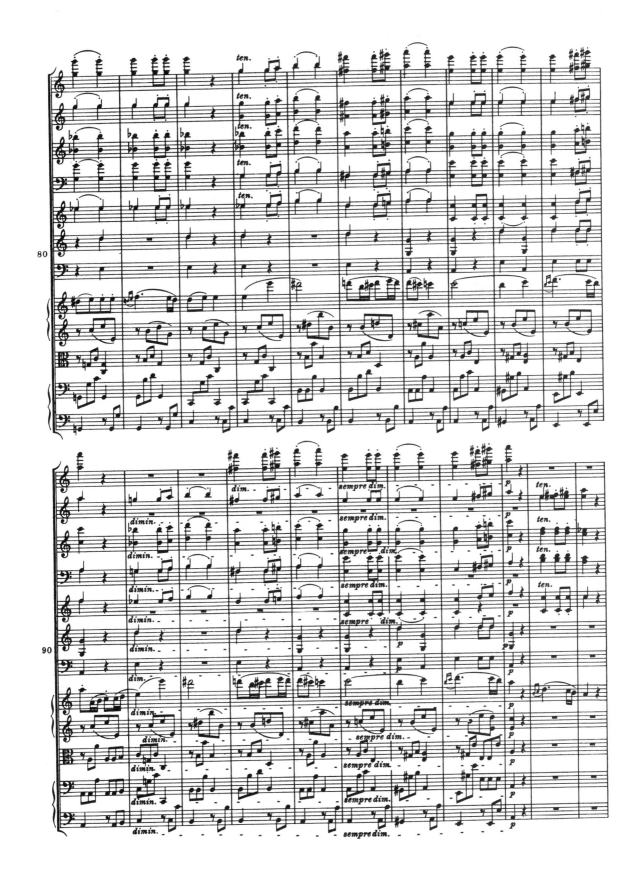

GENERAL QUESTIONS

TERMS

Before beginning this unit, make sure you know the meaning of each of the following terms. Check the Glossary at the end of the book for any term that is unfamiliar to you. As a further preliminary step, familiarize yourself with the form of this movement by studying the diagram below as you listen to a recording.

PITCH   chord mutation, sequence, parallel major, relative major, root movement

TEXTURE   countermelody, point of imitation, canon, fugato, stretto

FORM   variation form, rondo form, episode, development, transition

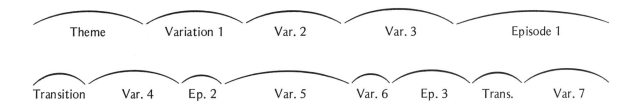

Theme	Variation 1	Var. 2	Var. 3	Episode 1

Transition	Var. 4	Ep. 2	Var. 5	Var. 6	Ep. 3	Trans.	Var. 7

GROUP 1

RHYTHM

1. The meter is (duple)(triple).

2. In the theme the basic duration is divided into (two)(three) parts.

3. The movement (is)(is not) based on a recurring rhythmic motive.

PITCH

1. The opening chord is

   a. M^5_3 b. M_6 c. m^5_3 d. m^6_4

2. The theme is based on

   a. triadic outlines
   b. repeated notes
   c. octave leaps

3. The first and last chords of the movement are (the same)(different).

TEXTURE

1. The texture of the theme is (chordal)(contrapuntal).

2. Variation 1

   a. is a figural variation
   b. adds a countermelody to the theme
   c. simultaneously states the theme and its inversion

FORM

1. The movement's two climaxes occur in

   a. Variations 3 and 6   c. Variations 3 and 7
   b. Variations 4 and 7   d. Variations 4 and 6

2. Material used in the first episode recurs with minor changes in

   a. Episode 2   c. Variation 5
   b. Episode 3   d. Variation 7

GROUP 2

RHYTHM

1. The division of the basic duration into three parts is a characteristic of the accompaniment in
   a. Variation 2   c. Variation 4
   b. Variation 3   d. Variation 7

2. The continuous division of the basic duration into four parts is first introduced in
   a. Variation 2   c. Variation 4
   b. Variation 3   d. Variation 6

PITCH

1. Without regard to the tonal center, each four-measure segment of the theme ends with which one of the following chord-class patterns?
   a. tonic-dominant   b. dominant-tonic   c. pre-dominant-dominant

2. The theme (does)(does not) contain a harmonic sequence.

3. The countermelody introduced in Variation 1 (is)(is not) totally diatonic.

TEXTURE

1. The variational process used in Variations 1 through 3 is
   a. the introduction of a countermelody that is continually restated in more elaborately ornamented versions
   b. the addition of a new textural layer in each section
   c. both (a) and (b)

2. Variation 2 is characterized by
   a. a continuous crescendo
   b. the first appearance of the trumpets and timpani
   c. both (a) and (b)

FORM

1. Without regard to the sustained chord at the opening, the theme comprises three units with (the same)(different) number(s) of measures.

2. The transitions at the ends of Episodes 1 and 3 are (the same)(different).

3. Which of the following can be regarded as a development section?
   a. Variation 4   b. Variation 5   c. Variation 6

GROUP 3

RHYTHM

1. The primary rhythmic motive of the theme is

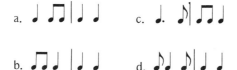

2. Episodes 1 and 3 use
   a. a three-part division of the basic duration
   b. a two-part division of the basic duration
   c. a three-part division of the basic duration in one layer of the texture and a two-part division in another layer

3. Episodes 1 and 3
   a. contain a rhythmic motive from the theme
   b. have no rhythmic relationship to the theme

<table>
<tr><td>PITCH</td><td>

1. Which of the following statements best describes the first unit of the theme?

   a. It cadences in the relative major.
   b. It cadences in the parallel major.
   c. It cadences in the same tonality and mode with which it opened.

2. Episode 1 begins with a change of (tonic)(mode) from Variation 3.
</td></tr>
</table>

PITCH

1. Which of the following statements best describes the first unit of the theme?

   a. It cadences in the relative major.
   b. It cadences in the parallel major.
   c. It cadences in the same tonality and mode with which it opened.

2. Episode 1 begins with a change of (tonic)(mode) from Variation 3.

TEXTURE

1. Variation 5 is based on the imitative principle of

   a. points of imitation   b. canon   c. fugato

2. At the end of the movement there (is)(is not) a stretto.

FORM

1. Which of the following represents the structure of the three units of the theme?

   a. xyx'   b. xyy   c. xx'y   d. xyy'

2. The last variation to use the countermelody is

   a. Variation 3   c. Variation 5
   b. Variation 4   d. Variation 6

3. The accompaniment figure of Variation 5 appears again in

   a. Variation 6   b. Episode 3   c. Transition 2

4. Variation 6 is an (abbreviated)(expanded) version of the theme.

GROUP 4

SCORE STUDY AND DISCUSSION

1. It has been mentioned that the theme and first three variations function as a single formal unit. Examine the changes in register, dynamics, texture, and orchestration in these four sections (measures 3-74). How do they interrelate to create this unit? Are there other formal units that are similarly defined?

2. Study the changes in timbre in the last variation. How do they affect the internal division of this section? Is there a pattern to their change?

PRACTICE DRILLS

RHYTHM

Tap or intone each of the following rhythmic patterns. Then play them on your instrument, being sure to give all notes their full value. (Perform two-line patterns either with another student or at the piano, playing one line while tapping or intoning the other, then reversing the procedure.)

1. (mm. 63-67)

2. (mm. 117-23)

3. (mm. 201-10)

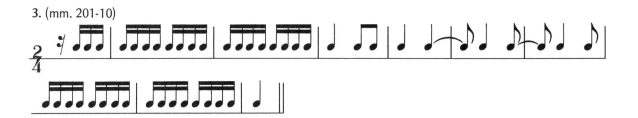

4. (mm. 75-78)

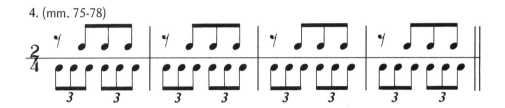

PITCH PATTERNS

Sing each of the following nonrhythmicized pitch-pattern excerpts, transposing up or down an octave as necessary to accommodate your voice range. Then play them on your instrument to check your accuracy.

1. (m. 52) **2.** (m. 76) **3.** (mm. 115-16) **4.** (mm. 112-13)

5. (mm. 182-83)

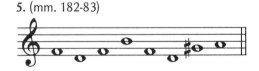

SONORITY TYPES

Play each of the following sonorities at the piano and sing each tone while the sonority is sounding. Play each sonority again, leaving out one of the tones; sing the missing tone. Repeat this procedure with each of the other tones.

Sing the sonority from the bass up and from the soprano down, using a close spacing to accommodate your voice range.

1. (m. 3) **2.** (m. 5) **3.** (m. 8) **4.** (m. 1) **5.** (m. 135) **6.** (m. 127)

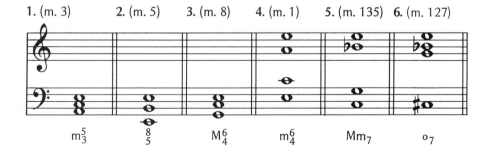

CHORD PROGRESSIONS

At the piano, play the chord progressions given on the bottom two staves while singing the vocalises given on the top staff. If you are not a keyboard player, arpeggiate the progressions on your instrument.

Without the aid of the piano, sing the vocalises and the progressions from the bass up and from the soprano down.

Analyze each progression as specifically as possible in the key given for it. You may analyze either by chord function class or by numeral.

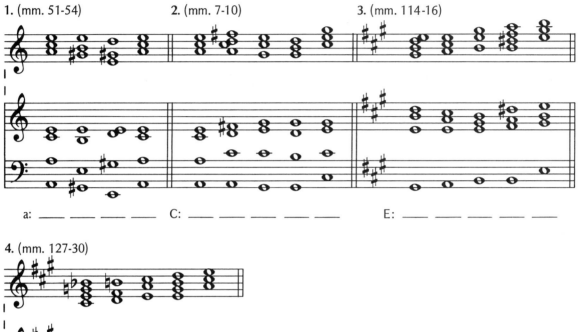

1. (mm. 51-54)   2. (mm. 7-10)   3. (mm. 114-16)

a: ___ ___ ___ ___   C: ___ ___ ___ ___ ___   E: ___ ___ ___ ___ ___

4. (mm. 127-30)

A: ___ ___ ___ ___ ___

DICTATION AND ANALYSIS

RHYTHM

You will hear one- and two-part excerpts from the movement. Notate the *rhythm only* of each excerpt. For each, the number of voice parts, the basic duration, and the suggested number of hearings, respectively, are given in parentheses.

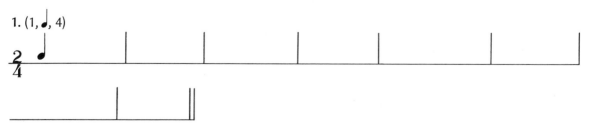

1. (1, ♩, 4)

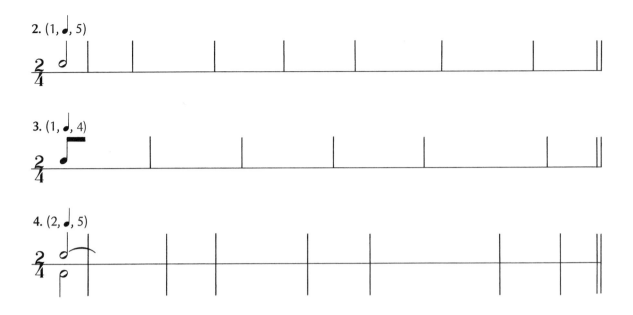

PITCH PATTERNS

Notate in whole notes the nonrhythmicized pitch-pattern excerpts that will be played for you. The suggested number of hearings is given in parentheses.

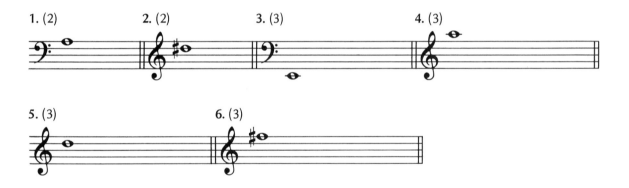

MELODIES

The melodies in this section are presented in two versions: (A) is a *basic* melody—that is, a reduced version of the original melody—and (B) is the *original* melody. Notate the basic melody on staff A and the original melody on staff B. The suggested number of hearings is given in parentheses. (For the original melody, this number is based on your having completed the basic melody first.)

COUNTERPOINT

The exercises in this section are presented in two versions: (A) is a *basic* counterpoint—that is, a reduced version of the original passage—and (B) is the *original* counterpoint. Notate the basic counterpoint on staff A and the original counterpoint on staff B. The suggested number of hearings is given in parentheses. (For the original version, this number is based on your having completed the basic version first.)

SONORITY TYPES

Each of the following items represents a sonority that you are to identify in two hearings. The number of voices in each sonority is given in parentheses.

You are given the highest (stem up) or the lowest (stem down) pitch for each sonority. Notate the other outer voice and as many of the inner voices as you can. Be sure to include any necessary accidentals.

Below each sonority, indicate its sounding chord quality, including inversion (for example, m_3^5, M_4^6, Mm_7, ϕ_5^6).

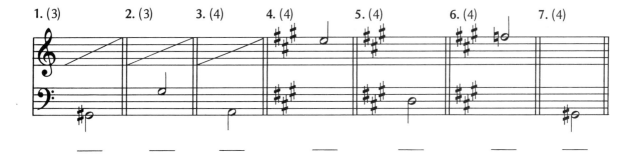

SELECTIVE LISTENING

NONCHORD TONES

In the following exercises you are given the rhythm of the upper voice of two excerpts from the movement. Each contains nonchord tones, the location of which is indicated by asterisks. From the following list, select the appropriate nonchord tone and place its letter beside the corresponding asterisk. The suggested number of hearings for each exercise is two.

a. passing tone   c. appoggiatura   e. escape tone
b. neighbor tone   d. retardation   f. suspension

1.

2.

TONAL CHANGE

You will hear two harmonic progressions in which tonal changes occur. For each, the first tonic is given. Add the letter name of the second tonic and the mode of the first and second key in each case. The suggested number of hearings for each exercise is two.

1. First tonic: A   first mode: ____
    Second tonic: ____   second mode: ____

2. First tonic: A   first mode: ____
    Second tonic: ____   second mode: ____

CHORD MUTATION

You are given the harmonic rhythm of a passage containing two progressions in which the chord quality changes while the chord root stays the same. Bracket these two mutations. The suggested number of hearings is two.

HARMONIC FUNCTION

1. Below you are given the rhythm of the top voice of an excerpt from the movement. Answer the following questions. The suggested number of hearings is two.

   a. A (tonic)(dominant) pedal is heard throughout most of the passage.

   b. The passage enclosed in the first bracket focuses on the (subdominant)(dominant) of the key.

   c. The passage enclosed in the second bracket focuses on the (subdominant) (dominant) of the key.

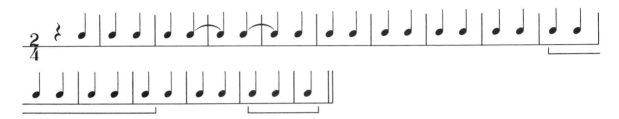

2. Below you are given the rhythm of a passage which begins on the tonic. Answer the following questions. The suggested number of hearings is two.

   a. The passage enclosed in the first bracket focuses on the (subdominant)(dominant) of the key.

   b. The passage enclosed in the second bracket is a harmonic sequence. The root movement within the sequenced pattern is up a perfect (fourth)(fifth).

HARMONIC PROGRESSIONS

Notate the outer voices of the modulating harmonic progression that will be played for you. The chord series I$^6_4$-V$_{(7)}$-I is used twice; bracket each appearance. Indicate the chord function class of the two chords above the asterisks. The harmonic rhythm and the opening pitches are provided. The suggested number of hearings is four.

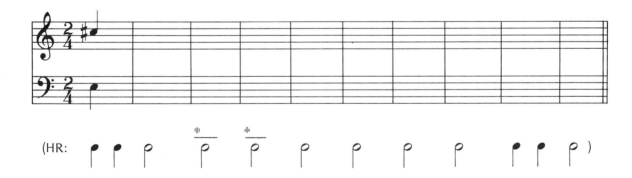

9

FRÉDÉRIC CHOPIN
(1810–1849)

Nocturne in F♯ Minor, Op. 48, No. 2

Chopin's F♯ Minor Nocturne, composed in 1841, belongs to a body of nineteenth-century piano music termed "character pieces." These short compositions have such titles as Capriccio, Bagatelle, Impromptu, etc., and are atmospheric in nature, being designed to evoke some particular mood or moods. Like many works of the genre, this Nocturne exhibits a rather simple formal scheme of ternary design (ABA). The work is typical of the composer in its use of chromatic harmony, colorful key relationships, and occasional rapid melodic figures. These figures are particularly obvious in the B section, where they momentarily interrupt harmonic progressions that continue over several measures. An additional point of interest is the implication of counterpoint by the single melodic line in the lower part of the texture of the A sections.

CHOPIN: NOCTURNE IN F♯ MINOR, OP. 48, NO. 2

GENERAL QUESTIONS

TERMS

Before beginning this unit, make sure you know the meaning of each of the following terms. Check the Glossary at the end of the book for any term that is unfamiliar to you.

RHYTHM   irregular division of the beat

PITCH   conjunct, disjunct, tonal region, chromatic third relation, thirteenth chord

FORM   ternary form, return, coda

GROUP 1

RHYTHM
1. The tempo of this composition (does)(does not) change.

2. The meter changes (once)(twice).

PITCH
1. The motion of the upper line of the A section is
   a. conjunct   b. a mixture of conjunct and disjunct

2. Which of the following patterns are prominent motives of the B section?

TEXTURE
1. The A section is primarily in a two-part texture. The lines are best described as
   a. equally important   b. a melody and a supporting accompaniment

2. The lower line of the A section is based on (broken chords)(scales).

3. The texture of the B section is (the same as)(different from) that of the A section.

FORM
1. The immediate repetition of phrases is an (important)(unimportant) formal procedure in the composition.

2. The form of this work is best described as
   a. ABA   b. ABA with coda   c. ABA'   d. ABA' with coda

GROUP 2

RHYTHM
1. The meters of the A and B sections are respectively
   a. $\frac{4}{4}, \frac{3}{4}$ b. $\frac{3}{4}, \frac{4}{4}$ c. $\frac{4}{4}, \frac{9}{8}$ d. $\frac{9}{8}, \frac{4}{4}$

2. In the accompaniment of the A section, the division of the basic duration is (duple) (triple); the division of the basic duration of the melody in the A section is predominantly (duple)(triple).

3. The B section at times uses quintuplets, sextuplets, etc. These appear on the (first) (last) beat of the measure.

PITCH

1. Measures 1 and 2 emphasize the (tonic)(dominant) harmony.

2. The contour of the accompaniment in the A section is

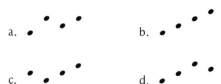

3. The melodic styles of the A and B sections are (similar)(contrasting).

TEXTURE

Which of the following statements is/are true?

    a. The work is imitative.
    b. The highest pitches of the work appear in the B section.
    c. The dynamic climax of the work appears in the B section.

FORM

1. When a phrase is immediately repeated, the repetition is (varied)(exact).

2. The coda is derived from the materials of

    a. the A section
    b. the B section
    c. both the A and the B sections

GROUP 3

RHYTHM

1. Which of the following motives is/are prominently used in the B section?

    a.   b.   c.   d.

2. Twice within the B section two measures of $\frac{3}{4}$ are structured so as to create the feeling of one measure of $\frac{3}{2}$. This is a result of

    a. registral change
    b. alternating between forte and piano
    c. pattern repetition

PITCH

1. Which of the following patterns represents the opening two measures of the upper voice?

2. The opening tonic of the B section lies a perfect (fourth)(fifth) below the closing tonic of the first A section.

3. The final chord of the work is (major)(minor).

TEXTURE

Which of the items listed below is/are present in this work?

    a. trills
    b. grace notes
    c. coloratura ornamenting of the melody

    d. monophony
    e. octave doubling of the melody
    f. extended passage in parallel thirds

FORM Complete the formal diagram begun for you below by showing the remaining internal divisions of the A, B, and A′ sections. Indicate the measure numbers of all divisions.

A   B   A′   Coda

a   b

GROUP 4

SCORE STUDY AND DISCUSSION

1. Variation is an important compositional procedure in much of Chopin's music. Examine the opening measures of the work; then trace their reappearance throughout. How is the material varied? Can you suggest a rationale for the positioning of the most elaborate variants?

2. The accompaniment in the A sections implies contrapuntal lines. On the staves below, rewrite the accompaniment from measure 3 through the first half of measure 10 to show this. Compare your version with those of other students. Is only one interpretation possible?

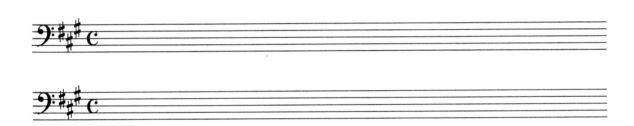

PRACTICE DRILLS

RHYTHM

Tap or intone each of the following rhythmic patterns. Then play them on your instrument, being sure to give all notes their full value. (Perform two-line patterns either with another student or at the piano, playing one line while tapping or intoning the other, then reversing the procedure.)

1. (mm. 1-3)

2. (mm. 103-05)

3. (mm. 95-100)

4. (mm. 43-45)

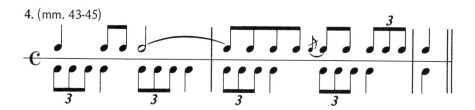

PITCH PATTERNS

Sing each of the following nonrhythmicized pitch-pattern excerpts, transposing up or down an octave as necessary to accommodate your voice range. Then play them on your instrument to check your accuracy.

1. (m. 3)   **2.** (m. 5)   **3.** (m. 9)   **4.** (m. 57)

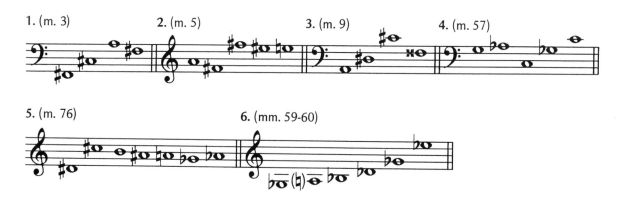

5. (m. 76)   **6.** (mm. 59-60)

SONORITY TYPES

Play each of the following sonorities at the piano and sing each tone while the sonority is sounding. Play each sonority again, leaving out one of the tones; sing the missing tone. Repeat this procedure with each of the other tones.

Sing the sonority from the bass up and from the soprano down, using a close spacing to accommodate your voice range.

1. (m. 57)   **2.** (m. 69)   **3.** (m. 57)   **4.** (m. 69)   **5.** (m. 65)

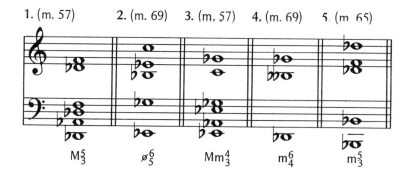

CHORD PROGRESSIONS

At the piano, play the chord progressions given on the bottom two staves while singing the vocalises given on the top staff. If you are not a keyboard player, arpeggiate the progressions on your instrument.

Without the aid of the piano, sing the vocalises and the progressions from the bass up and from the sporano down.

Analyze each progression as specifically as possible in the key given for it. You may analyze either by chord function class or by numeral.

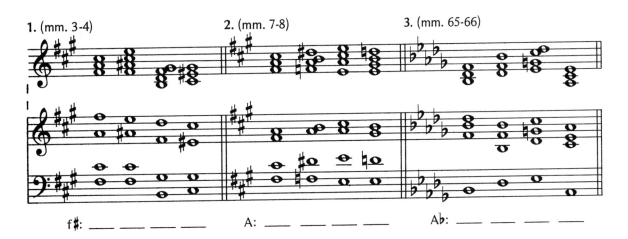

1. (mm. 3-4)   2. (mm. 7-8)   3. (mm. 65-66)

f#: ___ ___ ___ ___   A: ___ ___ ___ ___ ___   Ab: ___ ___ ___ ___

4. (mm. 119-20)

F#: ___ ___ ___ ___

DICTATION AND ANALYSIS

RHYTHM

You will hear one- and two-part excerpts from the work. Notate the *rhythm only* of each excerpt. For each, the number of voice parts, the basic duration, and the suggested number of hearings, respectively, are given in parentheses.

1. (1, ♩, 4)

2. (1, ♩, 6)

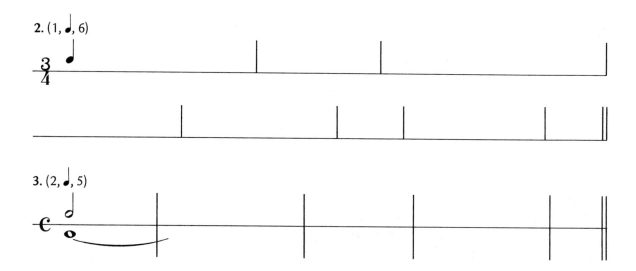

3. (2, ♩, 5)

PITCH PATTERNS

Notate in whole notes the nonrhythmicized pitch-pattern excerpts that will be played for you. The suggested number of hearings is given in parentheses.

1. (2) **2.** (2) **3.** (2)

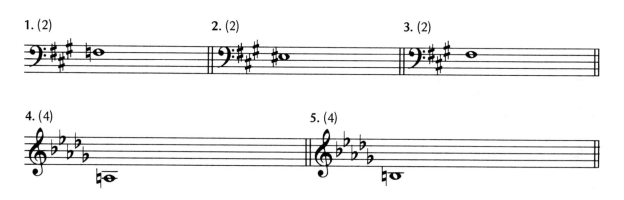

4. (4) **5.** (4)

MELODIES

The melodies in this section are presented in two versions: (A) is a *basic* melody—that is, a reduced version of the original melody—and (B) is the *original* melody. Notate the basic melody on staff A and the original melody on staff B. The suggested number of hearings is given in parentheses. (For the original melody, this number is based on your having completed the basic melody first.)

1. (3)

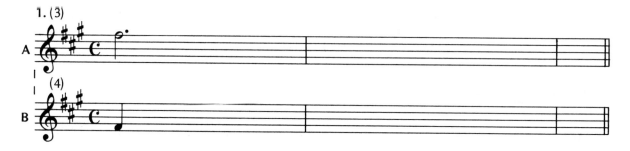

A

(4)

B

168   CHOPIN: NOCTURNE IN F♯ MINOR, OP. 48, NO. 2

COUNTERPOINT

The exercises in this section are presented in two versions: (A) is a *basic* counterpoint—that is, a reduced version of the original passage—and (B) is the *original* counterpoint. Notate the basic counterpoint on staff A and the original counterpoint on staff B. The suggested number of hearings is given in parentheses. (For the original version, this number is based on your having completed the basic version first.)

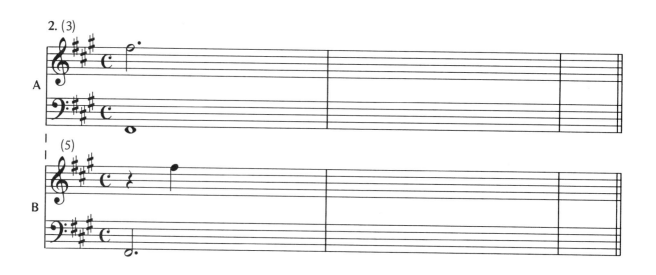

SONORITY TYPES

Each of the following items represents a four-voice sonority that you are to identify in two hearings.

You are given the highest (stem up) or the lowest (stem down) pitch for each sonority. Notate the other outer voice and as many of the inner voices as you can. Be sure to include any necessary accidentals.

Below each sonority, indicate its sounding chord quality, including inversion (for example, m$_3^5$, M$_4^6$, Mm$_7$, ϕ_5^6).

SELECTIVE LISTENING

NONCHORD TONES
In the following exercises you are given the rhythm of the upper voice of an excerpt from the work. It contains nonchord tones, the location of which is indicated by asterisks. From the following list, select the appropriate nonchord tone and place its letter beside the corresponding asterisk. The suggested number of hearings is two.

a. 9-8 suspension c. 4-3 suspension e. retardation
b. 7-6 suspension d. appoggiatura f. anticipation

TONAL CHANGE
Below you are given the rhythm of the upper voice of two passages that move rather rapidly through various tonal regions. The opening key and important cadences are indicated on the diagram. What tonic is in effect at each blank? The suggested number of hearings for each exercise is four.

1.

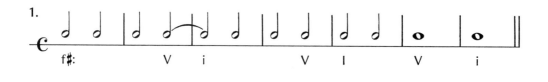

2.

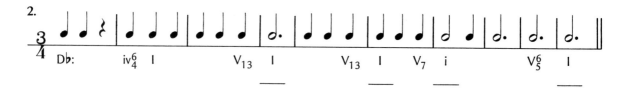

DOMINANT THIRTEENTH CHORDS
Below you are given the rhythm of an excerpt that contains five bracketed sets of chords with a dominant-tonic relationship. Put a checkmark under each bracket where the dominant function is a thirteenth chord. The suggested number of hearings is two.

CHROMATIC THIRD RELATION
Below you are given the harmonic rhythm of an excerpt that contains a chromatic third relationship. Bracket the two chords creating this relationship. The suggested number of hearings is two.

HARMONIC PROGRESSIONS

The exercises in this section are chordal versions of passages from the work. Notate the outer voices of each progression and add the specific numeral function of each chord that has a blank beneath it. For each chord where an asterisk precedes the blank, you need add only the chord function class. The harmonic rhythm (HR), the first numeral function, and the key are given for each exercise. The suggested number of hearings for each is five.

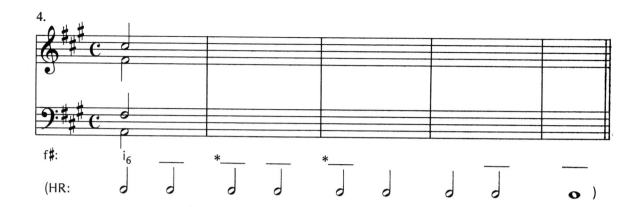

HUGO WOLF
(1860–1903)

Anakreons Grab

Among the various musical genres appearing at the beginning of the seventeenth century was the German song, or *lied*, for solo voice and accompaniment. The *lied* continued as a secondary means of expression for Classical composers such as Mozart and Beethoven, but attained its greatest importance with the Romantic composers in the nineteenth century—first in the songs of Schubert, and then in those of Schumann and Brahms. Hugo Wolf's *lieder*, written mainly within a ten-year span beginning in 1887, represent the culmination of this nineteenth-century period of development.

Anakreons Grab (Anacreon's Grave) was composed in 1888 and published two years later in a set of songs entitled *Goethelieder.* Goethe's text is an atmospheric description of the burial site of Anacreon, ancient Greek poet of the pleasures of wine and love. Here is a translation:

> Here where the rose blooms,
> Where the vines and laurel entwine,
> Where the turtledove coos,
> Where the grasshopper is glad,
> What grave lies here that all the gods
> Have so planted with green life?
> It is Anacreon's resting place.
> Spring, summer, and autumn
> Were enjoyed by the happy poet;
> He is shielded from the winter by the hill.

The work, which also exists in an orchestral version, is unified by a recurring broken-chord motive in the right hand of the piano part. In its treatment of dissonance and its chord vocabulary, the song employs a harmonic idiom which at times approximates that of Richard Wagner.

Sehr langsam und ruhig

Wo die Ro-se hier blüht, ___ wo Re-ben und Lor-beer sich schlin-gen, wo das Tur-tel-chen lockt. ___ wo sich das Grill-chen er-götzt, ___ welch ein Grab ist hier, das al-le Göt-ter mit Le- - - - - - ben schön be-pflanzt und ge

GENERAL QUESTIONS

TERMS

Before beginning this unit, make sure you know the meaning of each of the following terms. Check the Glossary at the end of the book for any term that is unfamiliar to you.

PITCH   accented dissonance, conjunct, pedal point, nonfunctional harmony

FORM   ostinato, return

GROUP 1

RHYTHM
1. The number of basic durations per measure is
   a. two   b. three   c. four   d. five
2. The meter is (simple)(compound).

PITCH
1. The first sonority is
   a. major   b. minor   c. diminished
2. The last sonority is
   a. major   b. minor   c. diminished
3. Accented dissonance is (insignificant)(important).

TEXTURE
Melodic interest is
   a. concentrated in the vocal part
   b. concentrated in the piano part
   c. distributed between the voice and the piano

FORM
1. At the opening of the song, vocal phrases are (one)(two) measures in length.
2. The phrase structure established at the beginning (is)(is not) maintained throughout.

GROUP 2

RHYTHM
1. The tying of a note into the following beat is (a prominent)(an insignificant) rhythmic device.
2. With ♩. as the basic duration, which of the following note values does *not* appear in the piano part?
   a. 𝅗𝅥.   b. ♩.   c. ♪   d. ♪

PITCH
1. Which of the following statements best describes the role of chromaticism in this work?
   a. There is no chromaticism.
   b. Chromaticism is present, but it is used sparingly.
   c. There is much chromaticism.
2. A (tonic)(dominant) pedal point leads into the final cadence.

TEXTURE
The relation of the piano part to the vocal line is primarily (imitative)(nonimitative).

FORM

1. At the beginning of the work, phrase endings in the vocal part are characterized by
   a. longer note values and/or rests   c. neither (a) nor (b)
   b. a descending second   d. both (a) and (b)

2. There is a kind of on-going quality to this composition that results from
   a. an ostinato in the piano part
   b. placing strong chords of resolution so that they often coincide with the beginnings of vocal phrases
   c. avoiding the vocal line's highest tone until the very end of the composition

GROUP 3

RHYTHM

1. Which of the following rhythmic motives is used in the first three vocal phrases?

2. The harmonic rhythm at the opening of the composition is

PITCH   Which of the following is/are prominent?
   a. seventh chords
   b. a passage based exclusively on minor triads
   c. successive chords with two or more common tones
   d. conjunct motion in the bass line

TEXTURE   Which of the following statements best describes the relationship of the piano part to the vocal line?
   a. The piano part always doubles the vocal line.
   b. The piano part occasionally doubles the vocal line.
   c. The piano part and the vocal line are completely independent.

FORM   This composition can be heard as falling into four sections, as shown by the simple diagram below. The following events appear in sections 2, 3, and 4. Match them with the measure numbers to which they correspond.
   a. return to the opening material
   b. change from functional harmony to nonfunctional harmony
   c. area of greatest tonal stability

GROUP 4

SCORE STUDY AND DISCUSSION

1. Examine the return of the opening material (measure 13ff.). Is thematic return coincidental with key return? Compare the vocal line at this point with the vocal line at the opening. What are the differences and similarities?

2. Study the succession of chords in measures 7-12. What sonorities are present? How do the lines move? Which chords are points of departure or arrival? What kinds of dissonance are used? What factors contribute to a feeling of tonal instability in portions of this passage?

PRACTICE DRILLS

RHYTHM

Tap or intone each of the following rhythmic patterns, then play them on your instrument, being sure to give all notes their full value.

1. (mm. 11-12)

2. (mm. 9-10)

3. (mm. 1-3)

PITCH PATTERNS

Sing each of the following nonrhythmicized pitch-pattern excerpts, transposing up or down an octave as necessary to accommodate your voice range. Then play them on your instrument to check your accuracy.

1. (mm. 11-12)   **2.** (m. 9)   **3.** (mm. 17-18)   **4.** (mm. 14-15)

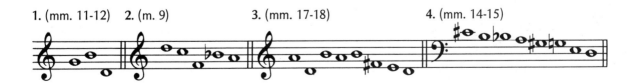

SONORITY TYPES

Play each of the following sonorities at the piano and sing each tone while the sonority is sounding. Play each sonority again, leaving out one of the tones; sing the missing tone. Repeat this procedure with each of the other tones.

Sing the sonority from the bass up and from the soprano down, using a close spacing to accommodate your voice range.

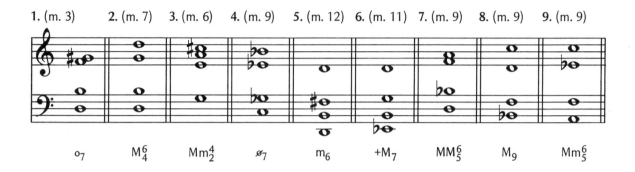

CHORD PROGRESSIONS

At the piano, play the chord progressions given on the bottom two staves while singing the vocalises given on the top staff. If you are not a keyboard player, arpeggiate the progressions on your instrument.

Without the aid of the piano, sing the vocalises and the progressions from the bass up and from the soprano down.

When the key is given, analyze the progression as specifically as possible in that key. You may analyze either by chord function class or by numeral.

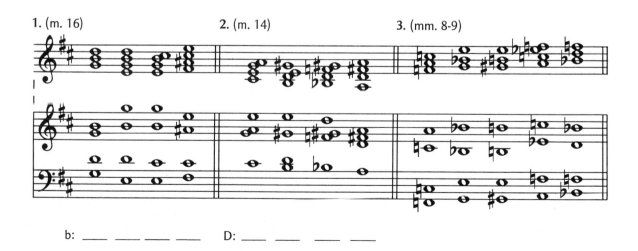

4. (mm. 9-10)

DICTATION AND ANALYSIS

RHYTHM

You will hear one- and two-part excerpts from the work. Notate the *rhythm only* of each excerpt. For each, the number of voice parts, the basic duration, and the suggested number of hearings, respectively, are given in parentheses.

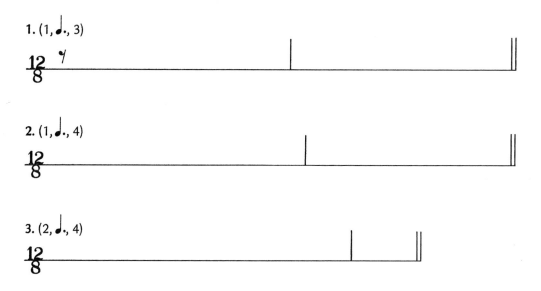

PITCH PATTERNS

Notate in whole notes the nonrhythmicized pitch-pattern excerpts that will be played for you. The suggested number of hearings is given in parentheses.

MELODIES

The melodies in this section are presented in two versions: (A) is a *basic* melody—that is, a reduced version of the original melody—and (B) is the *original* melody. Notate the basic melody on staff A and the original melody on staff B. The suggested number of hearings is given in parentheses. (For the original melody, this number is based on your having completed the basic melody first.)

1. (3)

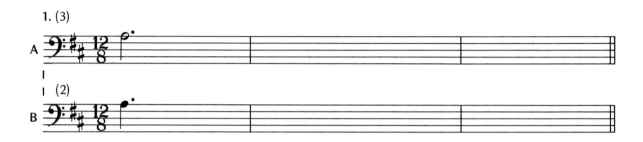

2. (3)

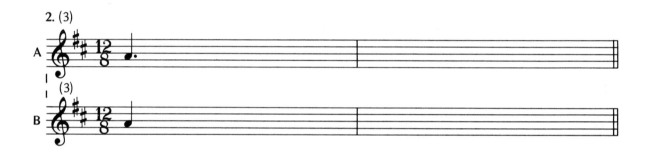

3. (3)

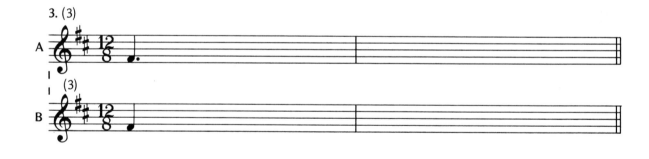

4. (3)

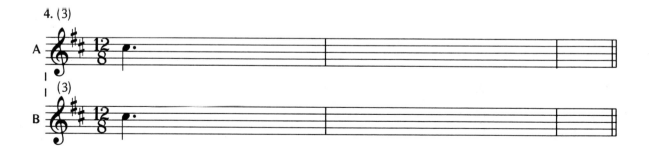

5. (4)

6. (5)

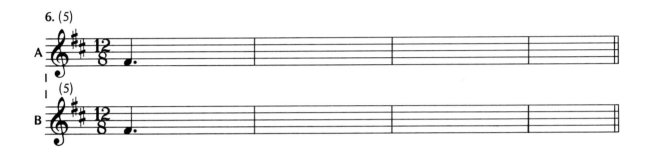

COUNTERPOINT

The exercises in this section are presented in two versions: (A) is a *basic* counter-point—that is, a reduced version of the original passage—and (B) is the *original* counterpoint. Notate the basic counterpoint on staff A and the original counterpoint on staff B. The suggested number of hearings is given in parentheses. (For the original version, this number is based on your having completed the basic version first.)

1. (4)

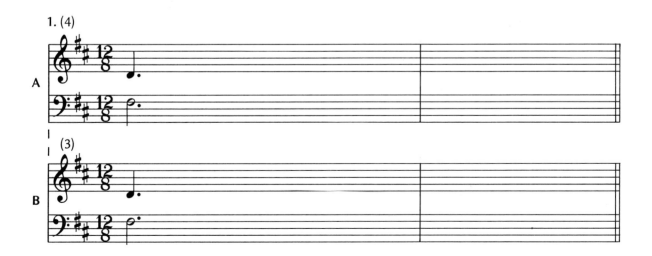

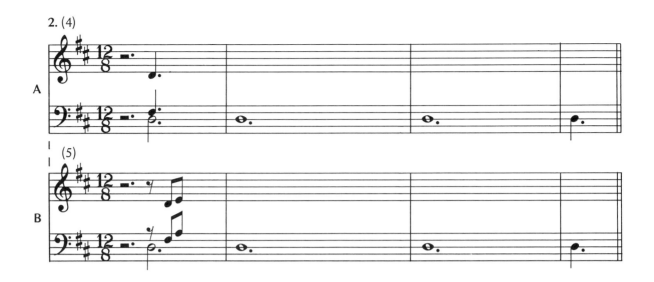

SONORITY TYPES

Each of the following items represents a four-voice sonority that you are to identify in two hearings.

You are given the highest (stem up) or the lowest (stem down) pitch for each sonority. Notate the other outer voice and as many of the inner voices as you can. Be sure to include any necessary accidentals.

Below each sonority, indicate its sounding chord quality, including inversion (for example, m, M, Mm$_7$, ϕ_5^6).

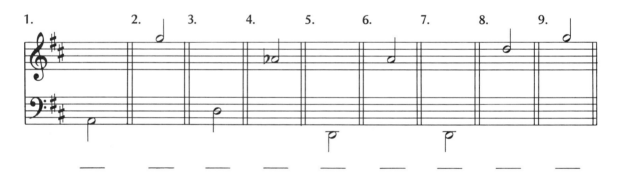

SELECTIVE LISTENING

NONCHORD TONES

In the following exercises you are given the rhythm of the upper voice of excerpts from the work. Each contains nonchord tones, the location of which is indicated by asterisks. From the following list, select the appropriate nonchord tone and place its letter beside the corresponding asterisk. The suggested number of hearings for each exercise is two.

a. passing tone   c. appoggiatura   e. escape tone
b. neighbor tone   d. retardation   f. suspension

HARMONIC FUNCTION

Below you are given the harmonic rhythm of an excerpt from the work. Under each note indicate whether the structural harmony functions as tonic (T), dominant (D), dominant substitute (Ds), diatonic pre-dominant (Pd), or chromatic pre-dominant (Pc). The suggested number of hearings is three.

HARMONIC PROGRESSIONS

A. You will hear two excerpts based on chromatic activity that bridges the distance between two root position triads. The root of the first triad is given. You are to give the mode of the first and second triads and the root of the second triad. The suggested number of hearings is three.

1. First triad root: F   first triad mode: _____
   Second triad root: _____   second triad mode: _____

2. First triad root: D   first triad mode: _____
   Second triad root: _____   second triad mode: _____

B. In the following excerpt a chord change occurs under almost every note in the upper voice, which is notated for you. Notate the bass voice and identify the chord quality, including inversions, where asterisks appear above the soprano. The suggested number of hearings is four.

C. The exercises in this section are chordal versions of passages from the work. Notate the outer voices of each progression, and add the specific numeral function of each chord that has a blank beneath it. For each chord where an asterisk precedes the blank, you need indicate only the sonority type. The harmonic rhythm (HR), the first numeral function, the key, and the suggested number of hearings (in parentheses) are given for each exercise.

1. (4)

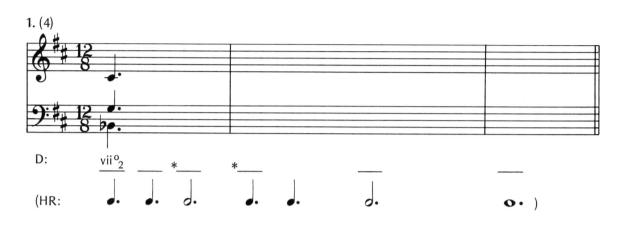

2. (5)

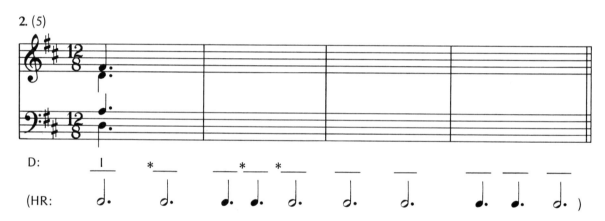

CLAUDE DEBUSSY
(1862–1918)

Prelude to the Afternoon of a Faun

This orchestral work was composed in 1894 and is one of the earliest examples of musical Impressionism. Debussy's literary inspiration was the poem *L'Après-midi d'un faune* (The Afternoon of a Faun) by the famous French poet Stephane Mallarmé. The Prelude is a beautifully flowing, highly integrated composition, characteristically Impressionistic in its interplay of instrumental colors, its rhapsodic lines, and its harmonic structure—a structure that by and large marks a departure from traditional functional relationships. Of particular interest here is Debussy's exploitation of motives and solo instruments.

20

2
1re FL.
SOLO
légèrement et expressif
p
2o
pp
CORS
4o
pp
1re HARPE
pp
8
2e HARPE
pp
2
pp
pp
Div.
pizz.
pp

DEBUSSY: PRELUDE TO THE AFTERNOON OF A FAUN

dans le mouv^t plus animé

GENERAL QUESTIONS

TERMS

Before beginning this unit, make sure you know the meaning of each of the following terms. Check the Glossary at the end of the book for any term that is unfamiliar to you.

RHYTHM   syncopation

PITCH   conjunct, disjunct, diatonic scale, whole-tone, ninth chords, thirteenth chords, added-tone chords

TEXTURE   imitation

FORM   section, sequence, variation

GROUP 1

RHYTHM

1. In this composition meter is

   a. not a perceivable feature
   b. constantly perceivable
   c. generally perceivable but obscured in some passages

2. The division of the basic pulse within the work is into

   a. two parts
   b. three parts
   c. as many as eight parts
   d. (a), (b), and (c)

PITCH

1. In the opening measures the melodic line spans the interval of a

   a. perfect fourth   b. perfect fifth   c. tritone

2. Which of the following patterns represents the melodic motive played by the solo French horn in the opening measures?

3. Which of the following statements is/are true?

   a. Melodic phrases in the work are generally of similar length.
   b. The melodic materials are essentially motivic.
   c. The melodic materials are essentially diatonic and conjunct.

TEXTURE

Compared to the orchestration in the Beethoven movement (Unit 8), Debussy's orchestration

   a. places more emphasis on solo instruments
   b. places more emphasis on the orchestra's color-producing capabilities
   c. makes more use of woodwinds
   d. makes less use of brass and percussion

FORM

Which of the following statements best describes the overall form of the work?

   a. There are three main sections of roughly equal length.
   b. There are four main sections, the last of which uses materials from the first.
   c. The work is continuous, with no reuse of materials in later sections.

GROUP 2

RHYTHM

1. Meter is obscured in portions of the composition by

   a. passages involving static harmony   c. complex counterpoint
   b. syncopation   d. lack of agogic (durational) accents

2. Harmonic rhythm in the work

   a. is never regular
   b. consists generally of two root changes per measure
   c. varies from section to section

PITCH

1. Which of the following scales appear(s) in the work?

   a. major   b. whole-tone   c. pentatonic   d. (a), (b), and (c)

2. In this work the dominant-tonic harmonic relationship

   a. plays no role   c. appears relatively infrequently, but
   b. appears frequently   plays an important role

TEXTURE

1. In this work the strings are used primarily to

   a. introduce melodic material   c. reinforce the texture, particularly
   b. accompany other instruments   at dramatic points within sections

2. Which of the following statements is/are true?

   a. Harp glissandi are used to add color to the work.
   b. No percussion instruments are used in this work.
   c. The only brasses used are trumpets and French horns.

FORM

1. Within the work, main sections are created by

   a. changes in instrumentation
   b. changes in accompanimental materials
   c. marked changes in tempo (e.g., from largo to allegro)
   d. changes in melodic material

2. Which of the following statements is/are true?

   a. Sequence does not appear in this work.
   b. Melodic units (motives, phrases) tend to be presented in pairs, that is, in a statement-repetition arrangement.
   c. Imitation does not appear in this work.

GROUP 3

RHYTHM

Which of the following statements about melodic passages is/are true?

   a. Rhythmic gestures often start with long notes and are followed by shorter ones.
   b. Rhythmic gestures often start with short notes and are followed by longer ones.
   c. Dotted rhythms and triplets are equally prominent.
   d. Notes tied across beats within measures are prominent.

PITCH

1. Sonority types in the work include

   a. major and minor triads   c. triads with added minor seconds
   b. Mm_7 d. triads with added major sixths

2. Root movements prominent in the work include

   a. major second   c. major and minor third
   b. tritone   d. (a), (b), and (c)

TEXTURE AND FORM

Below is a diagram of the main sections of the work. Fill it in by placing the letters of the following items in their appropriate locations. Place the letter of each melodic motive only where it *begins* a section. Indicate one instance only of items e, f, g, and h.

e. solo clarinet   g. sequence
f. solo violin   h. strong dominant-tonic cadence

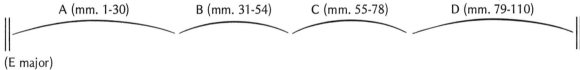

A (mm. 1-30)   B (mm. 31-54)   C (mm. 55-78)   D (mm. 79-110)

(E major)

GROUP 4

SCORE STUDY AND DISCUSSION

1. Study the score to determine the overall tonal structure. Here are some questions you might ask yourself: (a) Where are the major cadences and what tonality is in effect at each? (b) How does the tonality of Db in the third main section relate to the work as a whole? (c) Does the tonal structure of this work in any way resemble that of more traditional music? (You might compare the tonality of this work with that of the works by Bach, Haydn, Mozart, Beethoven, and Chopin in preceding units.

2. Within the first main section there are three ten-measure subsections, each of which begins with similar material. How does Debussy vary his materials at the beginning of each of these subsections to create contrast? Does variation as an organizing principle appear elsewhere in this work?

3. One of the characteristics of Impressionistic music is the smoothness of its flow. Study this work to see how Debussy has organized his materials so as to disguise the various underlying meters. Consider such factors as harmonic progressions, harmonic rhythm, durational patterns, and irregular divisions of the beat.

PRACTICE DRILLS

RHYTHM

Tap or intone each of the following rhythmic patterns. Then play them on your instrument, being sure to give all notes their full value. (Perform two-line patterns either with another student or at the piano, playing one line while tapping or intoning the other, then reversing the procedure.)

1. (mm. 1-2)

2. (mm. 55-59)

3. (mm. 28-30)

4. (mm. 102-03)

5. (mm. 22-23)

6. (mm. 44-46)

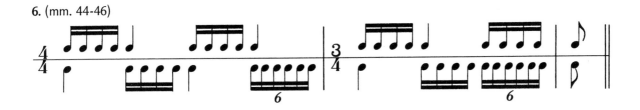

7. (mm. 31-32)

8. (mm. 104-06)

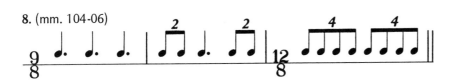

PITCH PATTERNS

Sing each of the following nonrhythmicized pitch-pattern excerpts, transposing up or down an octave as necessary to accommodate your voice range. Then play them on your instrument to check your accuracy.

1. (m. 37)   **2.** (mm. 14-15)   **3.** (mm. 1-2)   **4.** (mm. 15-17)

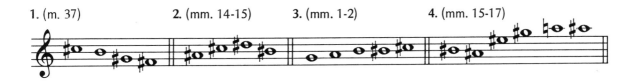

5. (m. 29)   **6.** (mm. 37-38)   **7.** (m. 47)

8. (m. 24)   **9.** (mm. 81-82)

SONORITY TYPES

Play each of the following sonorities at the piano and sing each tone while the sonority is sounding. Play each sonority again, leaving out one of the tones; sing the missing tone. Repeat this procedure with each of the other tones.

Sing the sonority from the bass up and from the soprano down, using a close spacing to accommodate your voice range.

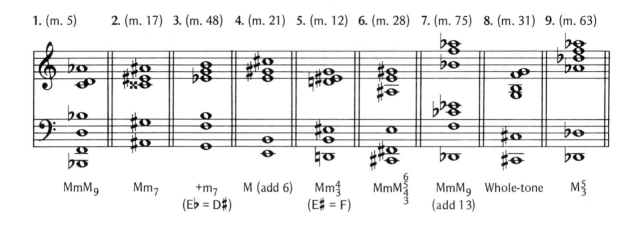

CHORD PROGRESSIONS

At the piano, play the chord progressions given on the bottom two staves while singing the vocalises given on the top staff. If you are not a keyboard player, arpeggiate the progressions on your instrument.

Without the aid of the piano, sing the vocalises and the progressions from the bass up and from the soprano down.

Analyze each of the chords in the progressions by sonority type and, wherever possible, indicate the chord root.

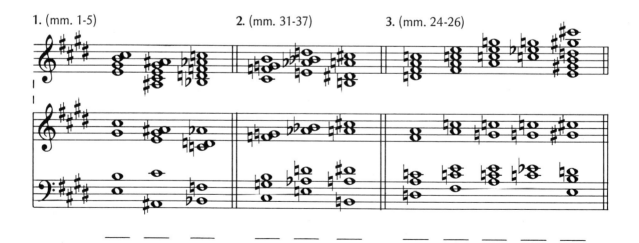

226   DEBUSSY: PRELUDE TO THE AFTERNOON OF A FAUN

4. (mm. 22-23)

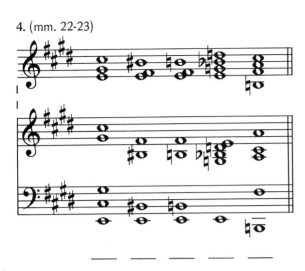

DICTATION AND ANALYSIS

RHYTHM

You will hear one- and two-part excerpts from the work. Notate the *rhythm only* of each excerpt. For each, the number of voice parts, the basic duration, and the suggested number of hearings, respectively, are given in parentheses.

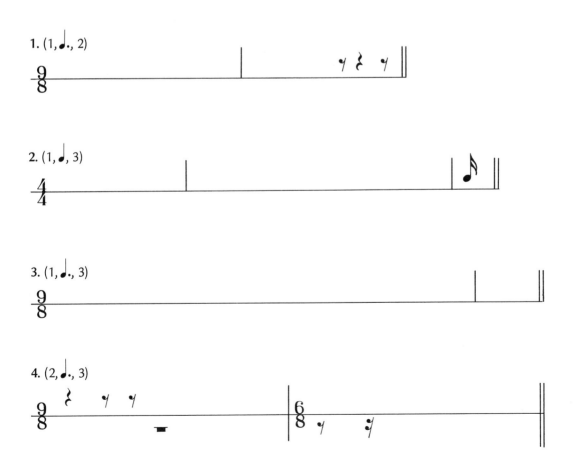

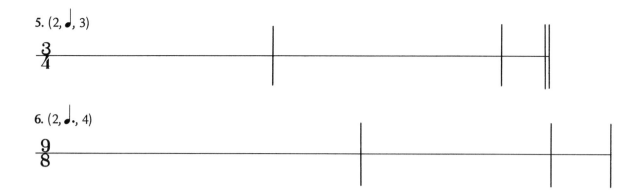

PITCH PATTERNS

Notate in whole notes the nonrhythmicized pitch-pattern excerpts that will be played for you. The suggested number of hearings is given in parentheses.

MELODIES

All but the first of the melodies in this section are presented in two versions: (A) is a *basic* melody—that is, a reduced version of the original melody and (B) is the *original* melody. Notate the basic melody on staff A and the original melody on staff B. The suggested number of hearings is given in parentheses. (For the original melody, this number is based on your having completed the basic melody first.)

1. (3)

SONORITY TYPES

Each of the following items represents a sonority that you are to identify in three hearings. The number of voices in each sonority is given in parentheses.

You are given the highest (stem up) or the lowest (stem down) pitch for each sonority. Notate the other outer voice and as many of the inner voices as you can. Be sure to include any necessary accidentals.

Below each sonority, indicate its sounding chord quality, including inversion (for example, m, M, Mm7, ϕ_5^6).

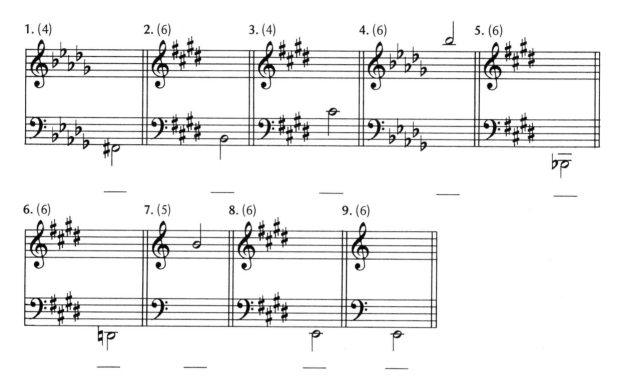

SELECTIVE LISTENING

Below you are given the rhythm of the outer voices of four excerpts from the work. Beneath each excerpt, place the letters of the accompanying items in their appropriate locations. In excerpts 1, 2, and 4, certain items will be heard more than once. The suggested number of hearings is given in parentheses.

1. (2) a. chord with added sixth   b. M$_3^6$ c. MmM9

2. (2) a. Mm7   b. parallel fifths   c. thirteenth chord (MmM9 plus 13)

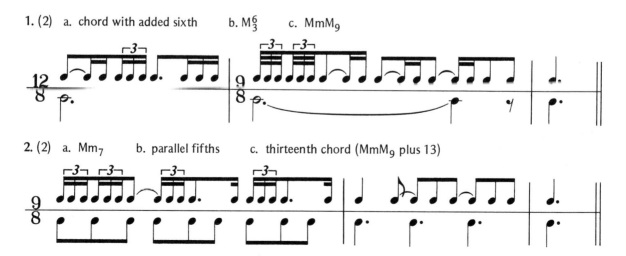

3. (3) a. all major triads (any inversion) in the first measure

b. all minor triads (any inversion) in the first measure

c. $\emptyset_7$

4. (3) a. chord with added sixth

Root relationship of consecutive chords by

b. tritone   c. major second   d. perfect fifth   e. semitone

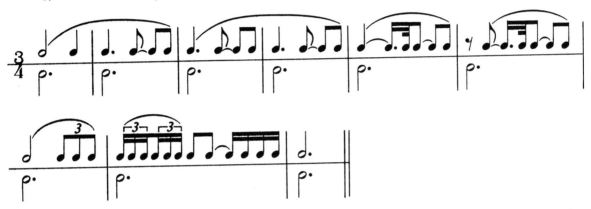

HARMONIC PROGRESSIONS

The exercises in this section are chordal versions (in most cases simplified) of passages from the work. Notate the outer voices of each progression and add the specific numeral function of each chord that has a blank beneath it. For each chord where an asterisk precedes the blank, add the root and sonority type, including inversion. The harmonic rhythm (HR), the first numeral function, the key (where applicable), and the suggested number of hearings are given for each exercise.

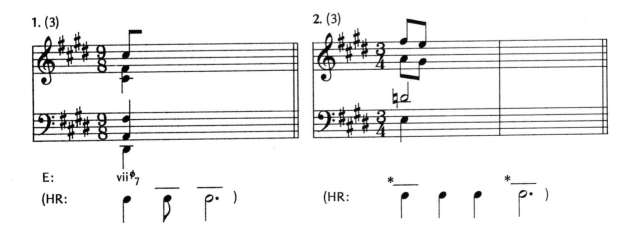

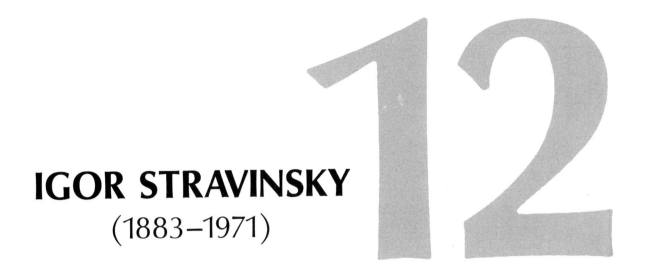

IGOR STRAVINSKY
(1883–1971)

Hymne
from SÉRÉNADE EN LA

"Hymne" is the first movement of *Serenade in A*, a four-movement piano work composed in 1925. As a point of departure for the compositions Stravinsky was writing in the 1920s and 1930s, he often drew on the procedures and sometimes even the actual music of earlier composers. This incorporation of a style from a previous musical period into a twentieth-century idiom is called Neoclassicism. One of the Neoclassical elements in "Hymne" is the use of tonality as an organizing factor, which many twentieth-century composers, Stravinsky included, had often abandoned in their earlier works.

The dominating melodic line of the movement doubtless accounts for its title; in this line, as in so many hymn tunes, there are long passages with a narrow range and few intervals larger than a third. In contrast to this melody is the bass line, which parodies the lower part of certain late Baroque compositions in its angular contours set to a constant rhythmic value. Stravinsky has combined these elements with his own language of phrase organization, sonority, and spacing to produce a unique style.

A ma femme

234   STRAVINSKY: HYMNE

*) Appuiez cette touche $(\overline{\overline{\Xi}})$
sans faire entendre le LA.

GENERAL QUESTIONS

TERMS

Before beginning this unit, make sure you know the meaning of each of the following terms. Check the Glossary at the end of the book for any term that is unfamiliar to you.

RHYTHM	hemiola
PITCH	sequence, whole-tone, pentatonic, pandiatonic, secundal chord, tertian chord, quartal chord, quintal chord
TEXTURE	canon, running bass, contrary motion, parallel motion

GROUP 1

RHYTHM

1. Which metronomic marking best represents the speed of the basic duration?

    a. 40   b. 60   c. 92

2. The meter of the opening measures is

    a. compound duple   b. simple duple   c. compound triple

3. During the course of this work the meter (does)(does not) change.

PITCH

1. Which of the following patterns represents the opening melodic motive?

2. Triadic outlining (does)(does not) occur in the lowest voice.

3. The melodic materials of the work are primarily based on

    a. recurring motives   b. nonrecurring motives

TEXTURE

1. The opening texture is

    a. homophonic   c. a balance between homophony
    b. contrapuntal   and counterpoint

2. How many textural layers are present at the opening of the work?

    a. two   b. three   c. four or more

3. During the course of this work the texture (does)(does not) change.

FORM

1. In the opening measures of the work the most important factor in phrase delineation is

    a. arrival at a harmonically stable point   c. dynamic change
    b. registral change   d. silence

2. The length of consecutive phrases is (the same)(different).

GROUP 2

RHYTHM

1. The opening rhythm of the upper voice is

2. With ♩. as the basic duration, the shortest note value prominently used is

a. ♩   b. ♪   c. ♪ (sixteenth)   d. ♪ (thirty-second)

3. The rhythm of the work is based primarily on

a. recurring motives   b. nonrecurring motives

PITCH

1. Throughout the composition the pitch motives of the highest line are (the same as) (different from) those of the lowest line.

2. Which of the following melodic devices is/are prominent?

a. sequence   b. interval expansion   c. phrase extension

3. Portions of this work are

a. whole-tone   b. pentatonic   c. pandiatonic

TEXTURE

Which of the following textural devices is/are present?

a. octave doubling   d. contrary motion
b. canon   e. streams of parallel intervals
c. running bass

FORM

1. A trill is used to signal the close of main sections. In how many places is this figure used?

a. two   b. three   c. four   d. five

2. Which of the following statements best describes the delineation of sections in this composition?

a. Textural changes are accompanied by changes in melodic and rhythmic patterns.
b. The same melodic and rhythmic patterns recur from section to section, but in varying textural contexts.

GROUP 3

RHYTHM

1. The underlying meter (is)(is not) consistently confirmed by the rhythmic groupings in the melody.

2. Which of the following rhythmic devices is/are present?

a. tying across the bar line   b. hemiola   c. double-dotted values

PITCH

1. On which of the following sonority types does the first phrase cadence?

a. M_3^5 b. M_3^6 c. m_3^5 d. m_4^6

2. On which of the following sonority types does the second phrase cadence?

a. M_3^5 b. M_3^6 c. m_3^5 d. m_4^6

3. On which of the following chord types does the third phrase cadence?

    a. secundal   b. tertian   c. quartal   d. quintal

TEXTURE

Which of the following kinds of parallel intervals is/are present?

    a. thirds   b. fourths   c. fifths   d. sixths

FORM

A measure outline of the movement is given below. Complete it by doing the following:

    a. Place "F" at the beginning of forte passages and "P" at the beginning of piano passages.
    b. Place ▬ at points of silence.
    c. Place "R" at the point where the two opening phrases return.
    d. Place " // " at points where streams of parallel intervals begin.
    e. Place "T" at points where trill figures appear.
    f. Place ♪ at the point where an extended passage of running sixteenth notes in the bass begins.

$1\frac{6}{8}$ 2   3   4   5 $6\frac{9}{8}$ $7\frac{6}{8}$ 8   9   10   11   12   13 $14\frac{9}{8}$

$15\frac{6}{8}$ 16   17   18   19   20   21   22   23   24   25   26   27   28

29   30   31   32   33   34   35   36   37   38   39   40   41 $42\frac{9}{8}$

$43\frac{6}{8}$ $44\frac{9}{8}$ $45\frac{6}{8}$ $46\frac{9}{8}$ $47\frac{6}{8}$ $48\frac{9}{8}$ $49\frac{6}{8}$ 50 $51\frac{9}{8}$ $52\frac{6}{8}$ 53   54   55

56   57   58   59   60   61   62   63 $64\frac{7}{8}$ $65\frac{6}{8}$ 66   67   68

69   70   71   72   73   74   75   76 $77\frac{9}{8}$ ⌒ $78\frac{6}{8}$ 79   80   81

GROUP 4

SCORE STUDY AND DISCUSSION

1. Examine measures 1 through 12. What tonic seems to be in effect for each phrase? How is the tonic established?

2. Study the organization of the first phrase, then study the rest of the movement to see how subsequent materials are related to it. Consider such factors as phrase contour, dominant rhythmic values, phrase duration, relation of voices and tonal organization. Are the phrases related in accordance with any consistent principle?

PRACTICE DRILLS

RHYTHM

Tap or intone each of the following rhythmic patterns. Then play them on your instrument, being sure to give all notes their full value. (Perform two-line patterns either with another student or at the piano, playing one line while tapping or intoning the other, then reversing the procedure.)

1. (mm. 52-53)

2. (mm. 74-77)

3. (mm. 62-65)

4. (mm. 45-47)

5. (mm. 3-6)

PITCH PATTERNS

Sing each of the following nonrhythmicized pitch-pattern excerpts, transposing up or down an octave as necessary to accommodate your voice range. Then play them on your instrument to check your accuracy.

1. (mm. 77-78)   2. (mm. 39-41)   3. (mm. 10-11)

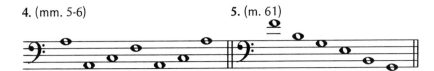

SONORITY TYPES

Play each of the following sonorities at the piano and sing each tone while the sonority is sounding. Play each sonority again, leaving out one of the tones; sing the missing tone. Repeat this procedure with each of the other tones.

Sing each sonority from the bass up and from the soprano down, using a close spacing to accommodate your voice range.

1. (m. 11)   **2.** (m. 27) **3.** (m. 26) **4.** (m. 57) **5.** (m. 65) **6.** (m. 77) **7.** (m. 78) **8.** (m. 43) **9.** (m. 1)

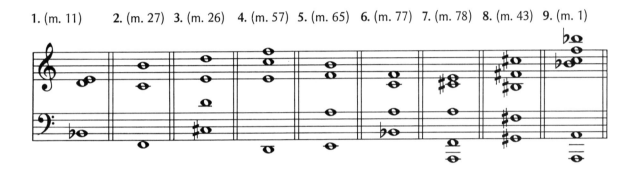

CHORD PROGRESSIONS

At the piano, play the chord progressions given on the bottom two staves while singing the vocalises given on the top staff. If you are not a keyboard player, arpeggiate the progressions on your instrument.

Without the aid of the piano, sing the vocalises and the progressions from the bass up and from the soprano down.

1. (m. 22)   **2.** (mm. 49-50)   **3.** (mm. 5-6)

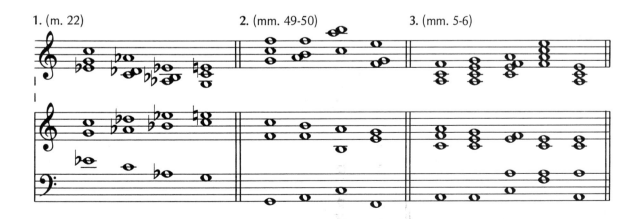

4. (mm. 39-41)

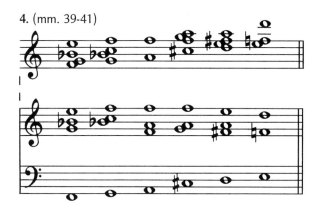

DICTATION AND ANALYSIS

RHYTHM

You will hear one- and two-part excerpts from the work. Notate the *rhythm only* of each excerpt. For each, the number of voice parts, the basic duration, and the suggested number of hearings, respectively, are given in parentheses.

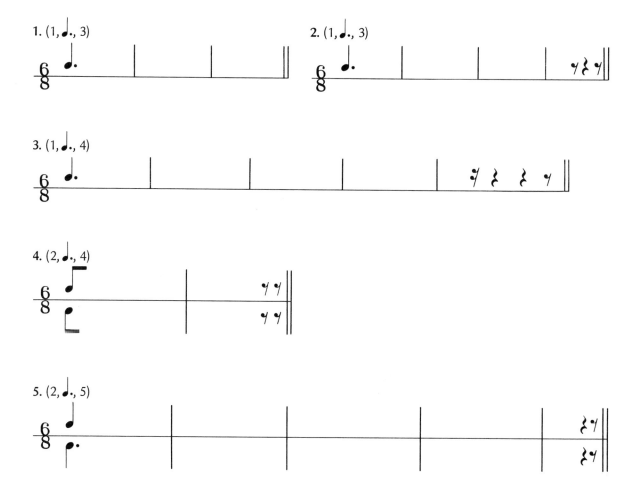

PITCH PATTERNS

Notate in whole notes the nonrhythmicized pitch-pattern excerpts that will be played for you. The suggested number of hearings is given in parentheses.

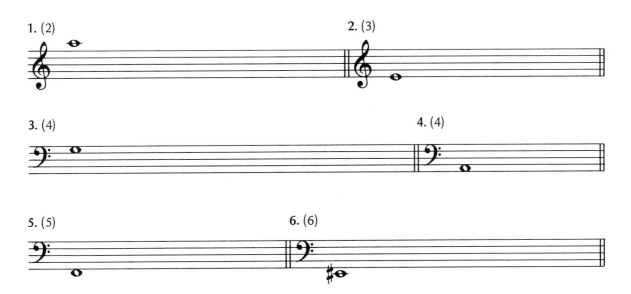

MELODIES

The melodies in this section are presented in two versions: (A) is a *basic* melody—that is, a reduced version of the original melody—and (B) is the *original* melody. Notate the basic melody on staff A and the original melody on staff B. The suggested number of hearings is given in parentheses. (For the original melody, this number is based on your having completed the basic melody first.)

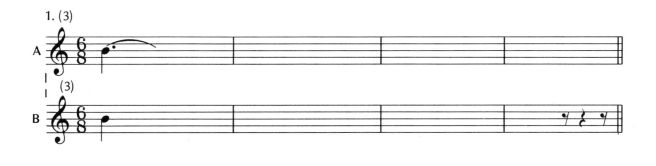

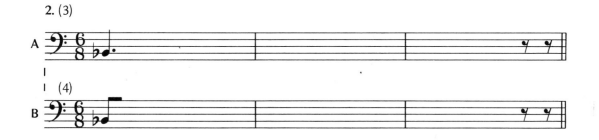

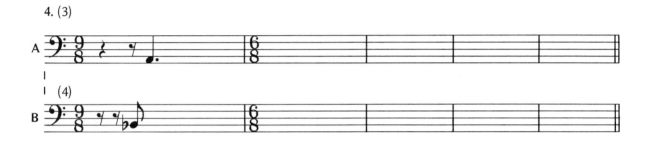

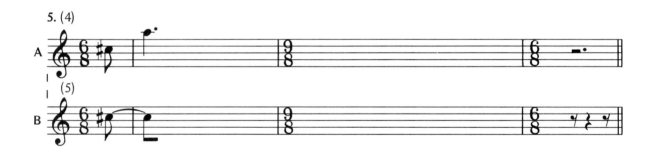

COUNTERPOINT

The exercises in this section are presented in two versions: (A) is a *basic* counterpoint—that is, a reduced version of the original passage—and (B) is the *original* counterpoint. Notate the basic counterpoint on staff A and the original counterpoint on staff B. The suggested number of hearings is given in parentheses. (For the original version, this number is based on your having completed the basic version first.)

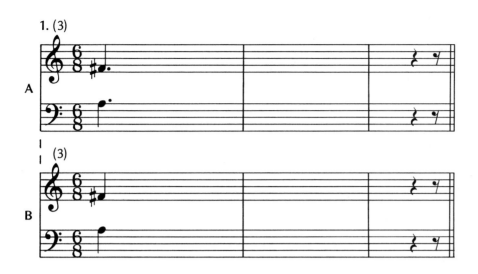

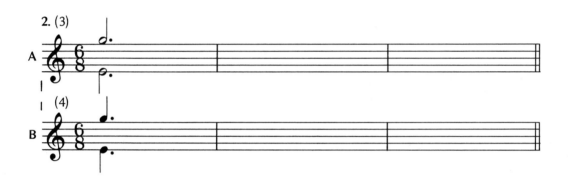

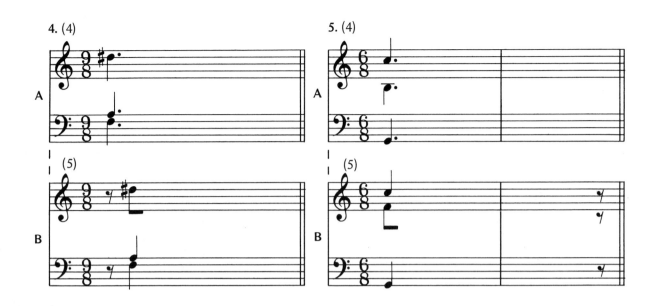

SONORITY TYPES

Each of the following items represents a sonority that you are to identify in two hearings. The number of voices in each sonority is given in parentheses.

You are given the highest (stem up) or the lowest (stem down) pitch for each sonority. Notate the other outer voice and as many of the inner voices as you can. Be sure to include any necessary accidentals.

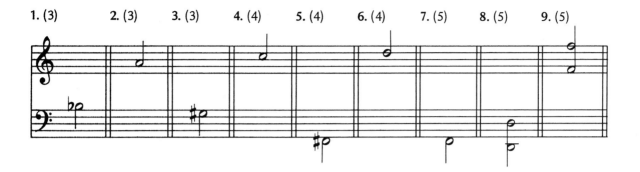

SELECTIVE LISTENING

NONCHORD TONES

In the following exercises you are given the rhythm of the outer voices of excerpts from the work. Each contains nonchord tones, the location of which is indicated by asterisks. From the following list, select the appropriate nonchord tone and place its letter beside the corresponding asterisk. The suggested number of hearings for each exercise is two.

a. neighbor tone   c. passing tone   e. 7-6 suspension
b. escape tone   d. appoggiatura   f. anticipation

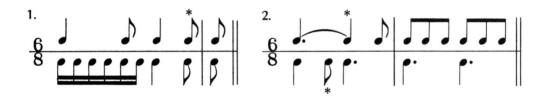

TONAL CHANGE

You will hear a harmonic progression in which a tonal change occurs. The first tonic is given. Add the letter name of the second tonic, the mode of the first and second keys and the means by which the change was effected (CT: common tone; CC: common chord; S: shift). The suggested number of hearings is two.

First tonic: E   first mode: ____
Second tonic: ____   second mode: ____   means: ____

HARMONIC PROGRESSIONS

SEVENTH CHORDS

Below you are given the harmonic rhythm of two harmonic progressions. At each blank indicate the type of seventh chord that is sounding, including inversion. The suggested number of hearings is three.

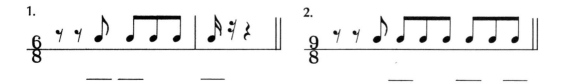

HARMONIC FUNCTION   Below you are given the rhythm of an excerpt from the work. At each blank indicate whether the sounding chord is pre-dominant (P), dominant (D), or tonic (T) in function.

BÉLA BARTÓK
(1881–1945)

13

Pihenö

from CONTRASTS

Contrasts (1938), for clarinet, violin, and piano, was commissioned by the American clarinetist Benny Goodman and is dedicated to him and Bartók's fellow countryman, the Hungarian violinist Joseph Szigeti. The lyrical second movement "Pihenö" (Rest) was an addition to the original design of two fast dances. It is cast in a rather free formal structure, which explores the idiomatic capabilities of the violin and clarinet in the context of added-tone chords and strictly controlled counterpoint. The piano has a subordinate role in the first half of the composition, where it plays trill figures and fragments of exotic scales. In the latter portion of the work the violin has a prominently reiterated *a'*, while in the final measures the coincidence of various contrapuntal elements results in sonorities of marked dissonance.

GENERAL QUESTIONS

TERMS

Before beginning this unit, make sure you know the meaning of each of the following terms. Check the Glossary at the end of the book for any term that is unfamiliar to you.

RHYTHM	irregular division of the beat, polymeter (successive and simultaneous)
PITCH	cross-relation, added-tone chord, pentatonic, whole-tone, Phrygian scale, Lydian scale, Locrian scale
TEXTURE	contrary motion, similar motion, parallel motion, oblique motion

GROUP 1

RHYTHM

1. In the opening measures the violin and the clarinet (do)(do not) have the same rhythm.

2. During the course of the movement the tempo (does)(does not) change.

PITCH

1. Generally speaking, the melodic lines are based on (recurring)(nonrecurring) pitch motives.

2. The scalar basis of the movement as a whole is

   a. pentatonic   b. whole-tone   c. Aeolian (natural minor)   d. chromatic

TEXTURE

1. What is the contrapuntal relationship between the violin and clarinet at the beginning of the movement?

   a. similar motion   c. parallel motion
   b. contrary motion   d. oblique motion

2. In the interior of the movement an imitative passage occurs between the

   a. piano and violin   c. the upper and lower voices of the piano
   b. piano and clarinet   d. none of these

FORM

1. Sectionalization results from changes in

   a. dynamics   b. texture   c. tempo   d. all of these

2. Which of the following statements best describes the conclusion of this movement?

   a. It is a modified return to the opening material.
   b. It is an exact return to the opening material.
   c. The opening material does not return in the movement's conclusion.

GROUP 2

RHYTHM

1. The opening rhythm is

   a.   c.

   b.   d.

2. Which of the following statements best describes the metric organization of this movement?

    a. There is no change of meter.

    b. The movement is based on successive polymeter, except for one extended passage in a slow sextuple meter.

    c. The movement is based on simultaneous polymeter.

PITCH

1. What is the opening harmonic interval?

    a. minor third   b. major third   c. minor sixth   d. major sixth

2. The final sonority of the movement (including the pizzicato in the violin) is

    a. mM_7 b. mm_7 c. ϕ_7 d. Mm_7

TEXTURE

Considering the movement as a whole, which statement best describes the relationship of the instruments to one another?

    a. Generally the style of writing is different for each instrument.

    b. All three instrumental parts are written in similar styles.

    c. Often the violin and clarinet parts are in similar styles while the piano part is in a different style.

FORM

1. Throughout the work phrases are generally of (the same)(different) length(s).

2. Within the main sections Bartók uses (exact)(varied) repetition.

GROUP 3

RHYTHM

1. Where in the movement does the fastest tempo appear?

    a. at the beginning   b. in the middle   c. at the end

2. Toward the end of the movement the piano plays a

    a. 2-against-3 rhythm   b. 3-against-4 rhythm   c. 3-against-5 rhythm

PITCH

1. Which of the following patterns represents the beginning of the clarinet line?

2. The opening duet for violin and clarinet (does)(does not) use cross relations.

3. Which of the following items appear(s)?

    a. the tritone used as a prominent melodic interval

    b. a motive based on a minor seventh

    c. a melodic idea based on interval expansion and contraction

TEXTURE

1. Which of the following instrumental techniques is/are used by the violin?

    a. harmonics   b. pizzicato   c. tremolo   d. double stops   e. mute

2. In the piano part, linear elements are frequently reinforced by a duplication at the interval of a

    a. minor second   b. perfect fifth   c. minor seventh   d. perfect octave

FORM	Rearrange the following events in order of their initial appearance in the movement.

a. tremolo in violin and trill in clarinet
b. extended use of contrary motion in the upper and lower voices of the piano
c. piano imitation of clarinet figure
d. extended use of contrary motion in the violin and clarinet
e. chromatically ascending perfect fifths in the violin
f. "give-and-take" contrapuntal relationship between the violin and clarinet
g. pizzicato note in the violin
h. the following violin passage:

i. the following clarinet passage:

GROUP 4

SCORE
STUDY
AND
DISCUSSION

1. In measures 11—14 the piano plays three descending pentachords in grace notes. On what scale is each based?

2. Several passages use contrary motion. Locate them in the score and describe the specific intervallic structure of each line. Then describe specifically the contrapuntal relationship between the lines.

3. In this movement varied repetition is an important aspect of the melodic organization. Describe the variational procedures used in the violin part.

4. Bartok apparently considered the movement to consist of five sections—note the indications of timing in measures 18, 28, 35, 44, and at the end. Study the internal structure of each of these in order to determine how they differ. Do you hear the separate sections as such?

PRACTICE DRILLS

RHYTHM

Tap or intone each of the following rhythmic patterns. Then play them on your instrument, being sure to give all notes their full value. (Perform two-line patterns either with another student or at the piano, playing one line while tapping or intoning the other, then reversing the procedure.)

1. (mm. 36-37)

PITCH PATTERNS

Sing each of the following nonrhythmicized pitch-pattern excerpts, transposing up or down an octave as necessary to accommodate your voice range. Then play them on your instrument to check your accuracy.

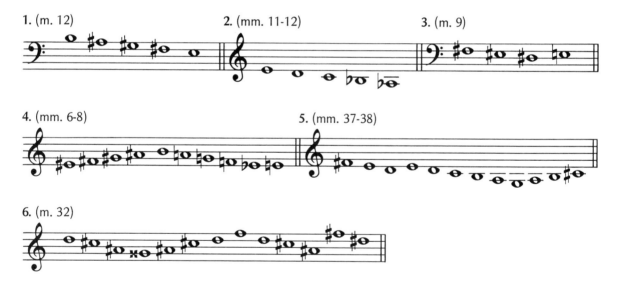

SONORITY TYPES

Play each of the following sonorities at the piano and sing each tone while the sonority is sounding. Play each sonority again, leaving out one of the tones; sing the missing tone. Repeat this procedure with each of the other tones.

Sing the sonority from the bass up and from the soprano down, using a close spacing to accommodate your voice range.

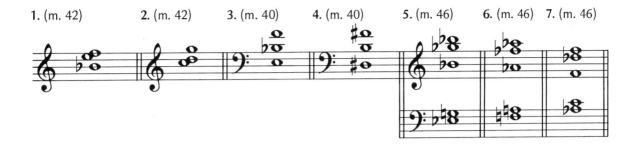

CHORD PROGRESSIONS

At the piano, play the following chord progressions. If you are not a keyboard player, arpeggiate the progressions on your instrument. Without the aid of the piano, sing the progressions from the bass up and from the soprano down, using a close spacing to accommodate your voice range.

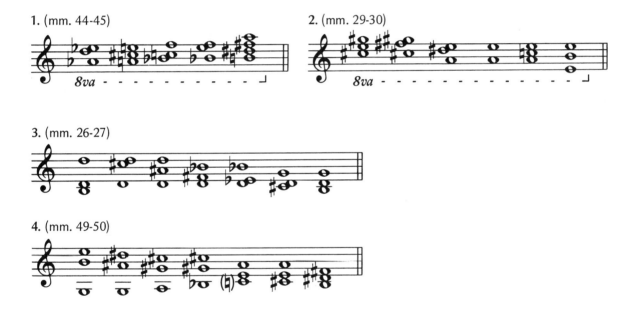

DICTATION AND ANALYSIS

RHYTHM

You will hear one- and two-part excerpts from the movement. Notate the *rhythm only* of each excerpt. For each, the number of voice parts, the basic duration, and the suggested number of hearings, respectively, are given in parentheses.

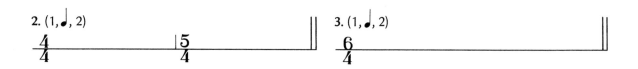

PITCH PATTERNS

Notate in the whole notes the nonrhythmicized pitch-pattern excerpts that will be played for you. The suggested number of hearings is given in parentheses.

MELODIES

The melodies in this section are presented in two versions: (A) is a *basic* melody—that is, a reduced version of the original melody—and (B) is the *original* melody. Notate the basic melody on staff A and the original melody on staff B. The suggested number of hearings is given in parentheses. (For the original melody, this number is based on your having completed the basic melody first.)

The exercises in this section are presented in two versions: (A) is a *basic* counterpoint—that is, a reduced version of the original passage—and (B) is the *original* counterpoint. Notate the basic counterpoint on staff A and the original counterpoint on staff B. The suggested number of hearings is given in parentheses. (For the original version, this number is based on your having completed the basic version first.)

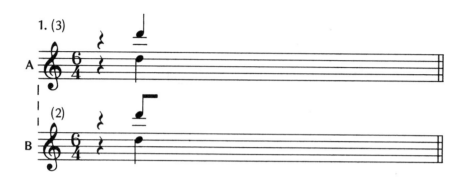

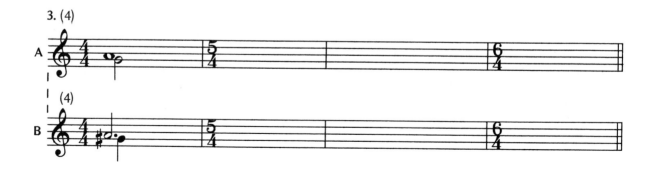

SONORITY TYPES

Each of the following items represents a sonority that you are to identify in two hearings. The number of voices in each sonority is given in parentheses.

You are given the highest (stem up) or the lowest (stem down) pitch for each sonority. Notate the other outer voice and as many of the inner voices as you can. Be sure to include any necessary accidentals. As an optional extra step, indicate the interval makeup of items 1 through 4 in semitone notation; you will find a description of the procedure in Unit 14, page 271.

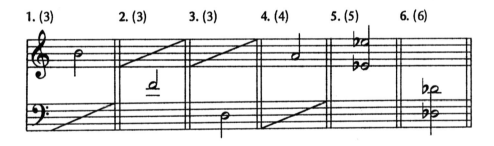

SELECTIVE LISTENING

INTERVALS   You will hear a passage containing two textural layers moving in contrary motion. Both layers consistently use which of the following harmonic intervals?

      a. minor third   b. major third   c. perfect fourth   d. perfect fifth

SONORITY TYPES   Listen three times to the five-chord harmonic progression that will be played for you. Answer the following questions:

1. The harmonic interval between the outer voices of each chord is a

      a. perfect fourth   b. perfect fifth   c. minor sixth   d. major sixth

2. Which of the five sonorities is/are major?

      a. chord 1   b. chord 2   c. chord 3   d. chord 4   e. chord 5

3. How many times is the following chord structure used:

minor second + tritone ─ perfect fifth

a. none   b. once   c. twice   d. three times

ADDED-TONE CHORDS

A six-chord harmonic progression will be played for you. Each chord contains a root-position major or minor triad and an "added" tone. Listen once for each of the following questions:

1. Which chord contains both a major third and a minor third above the lowest tone?

   a. chord 1   c. chord 3   e. chord 5
   b. chord 2   d. chord 4   f. chord 6

2. Which of the *remaining* chords is/are based on a root-position minor triad?

   a. chord 1   c. chord 3   e. chord 5
   b. chord 2   d. chord 4   f. chord 6

3. Which of the six chords contain(s) a minor sixth above the lowest tone?

   a. chord 1   c. chord 3   e. chord 5
   b. chord 2   d. chord 4   f. chord 6

4. Which of the six chords contain(s) a minor second above the lowest tone?

   a. chord 1   c. chord 3   e. chord 5
   b. chord 2   d. chord 4   f. chord 6

5. Which of the six chords contain(s) a tritone above the lowest tone?

   a. chord 1   c. chord 3   e. chord 5
   b. chord 2   d. chord 4   f. chord 6

6. Which of the following patterns represents the bass line of this progression?

a.   b.   c.   d.

LUIGI DALLAPICCOLA
(b. 1904)

"Simbolo" and "Fregi"
from QUADERNO MUSICALE DI ANNALIBERA

Dallapiccola's *Quaderno musicale di Annalibera* (Annalibera's Musical Notebook) was composed in 1952 for the Pittsburgh International Contemporary Music Festival, where it was given its first performance by the American composer-pianist Vincent Persichetti. Consisting of eleven pieces, the work is described by its composer as a set of variations, and, in fact, the title of the 1954 orchestral version is *Variations for Orchestra*. The work alludes to earlier music, in particular to the music of J. S. Bach, with the title mirroring that of Bach's *Musical Notebook for Anna Magdalena Bach*. Dallapiccola's reverence for Bach is especially evident in the motive of "Simbolo" (E♭, D, F, E♮, bars 2–5), which is a transposition of the pitch equivalents of the letters in Bach's name: B♭—A—C—B♮ (H equaling B♮ in German terminology). Further, the techniques and materials of *Quaderno*, especially the counterpoint, derive in spirit from earlier periods, though never departing from a thoroughly contemporary mode of expression.

Quaderno is one of a large number of twentieth-century compositions in which the organizing principle is the *twelve-tone* (or *serial*) method developed by Arnold Schoenberg around 1923. In this method, all twelve tones of the chromatic scale are arranged in a particular order. This series of tones is called the *basic set* or *row*, and in its original ordering (as in the top line of the first three and a half bars of "Fregi"), it is often called the *prime* (P) form.

The basic set can be manipulated in various ways: each tone can appear in any octave and can be enharmonically spelled, and the set as a whole can be transposed to begin on any degree of the chromatic scale. Further, the set can appear in *retrograde* (R), in reverse order; in *inversion* (I), with inverted intervals; and in *retrograde inversion* (RI), in inverted form in reverse order. Each of these forms can also begin on any degree of the chromatic scale. Thus, potentially, there are 48 different versions of one basic set—four forms in twelve transpositions each. Generally, only one basic set is used in a composition, with all linear and vertical pitch combinations derived from it and its various forms.

N. 1 - SIMBOLO

Reprinted by permission of Edizioni Suvini Zerboni, Milan.

N. 6 - FREGI

Molto lento; con espressione parlante (♪=76)

1 min. 10 secondi

TERMS

Before beginning this unit, make sure you know the meaning of each of the following terms. Check the Glossary at the end of the book for any term that is unfamiliar to you.

RHYTHM	syncopation, motive, diminution
PITCH	added-tone chords
TEXTURE	ostinato
FORM	section, return

TWELVE-TONE DRILLS

The following exercises are provided to acquaint you with the basic set of *Quaderno* and with its diad (two-tone), trichord (three-tone), and tetrachord (four-tone) subsets.

BASIC SET

Example 1 shows the basic set (P_0) and three of its transformations (I_{10}, R_0, RI_{10}). For simplicity, all the tones have been notated within a single octave.

Example 1†

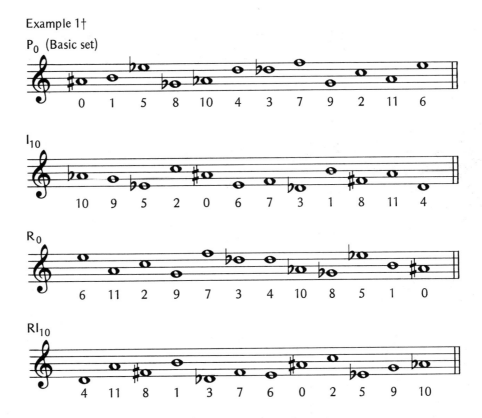

†In all the nonrhythmicized examples and excerpts in this unit, an accidental applies only to the note that it immediately precedes.

When the basic set for a work has been determined, its first tone may be numbered zero and all other tones numbered by their semitone distance *above* zero. Thus A♯–B becomes 0–1, A♯–E♭ becomes 0–5, A♯–G♭ becomes 0–8, and so on. The index numbers associated with the P and I forms refer to the tones on which these forms *begin* relative to zero (A♯ in this work). For R forms, the index numbers refer to the tones on which the forms *end*. Thus R_0 is the retrograde of P_0, and RI_{10} is the retrograde of I_{10}.

Sing these forms and play them on the piano.

DIADS

A fundamental principle of twelve-tone composition is that any tone of the set can appear in any octave. Thus, the inversion and compounding of intervals formed by successive tones is frequent. What remains constant in any such interval, no matter what its span (the distance between the highest and lowest tones), is its *interval class* (IC). An interval class comprises an interval and its inversion (or complement). There are six interval classes:

IC:	1	2	3	4	5	6
Intervals:	m2/M7	M2/m7	m3/M6	M3/m6	P4/P5	+4/o5

The white-note diads in Example 2 are those formed by the six successive pairs of tones in the P_0 and I_{10} set forms. The black-note diads are their complements. Interval classes are given above the example and intervals (in semitones), below.

Example 2

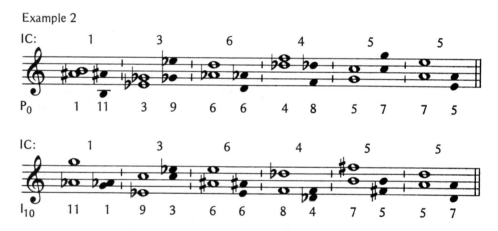

Sing the diads from the bottom up and from the top down and play them on the piano. For retrograde forms, reverse the order in the forms shown.

TRICHORDS

Example 3 shows the trichords formed by the four successive three-tone groups in the set forms P_0 and I_{10}. The chords in brackets are common tertian sonorities to which the trichords can be related.

Example 3

I_{10} $\frac{5}{4}$ MM_7 $\frac{8}{6}$ Mm_7 $\frac{10}{4}$ Mm_7 $\frac{7}{4}$

The numbers below each chord indicate the interval makeup in semitones measured above the lowest tone. (For intervals larger than the major seventh [11], simple interval equivalents are used with primes to indicate the degree of compounding. Thus an octave becomes 0′, a minor ninth becomes 1′, and so on.)

Note in the example that the corresponding trichords within the P and I forms contain the same intervals, though the internal structure is changed.

Sing the trichords from the bottom up and from the top down, and play them on the piano. For retrograde forms, reverse the order of the trichords in the forms given.

TETRACHORDS

Example 4 shows the tetrachords formed by the three successive four-tone groups in the set forms P_0 and I_{10}. Note that each tetrachord contains a major, a minor, or a diminished triad, and that each chord has the same span.

Example 4

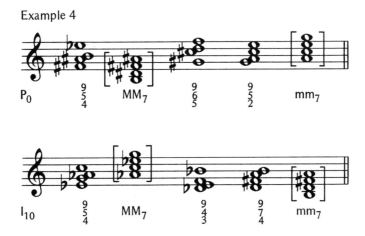

P_0 $\frac{9}{5}{4}$ MM_7 $\frac{9}{6}{5}$ $\frac{9}{5}{2}$ mm_7

I_{10} $\frac{9}{5}{4}$ MM_7 $\frac{9}{4}{3}$ $\frac{9}{7}{4}$ mm_7

Sing the tetrachords from the bottom up and from the top down, and play them on the piano. For additional practice, rearrange the trichords and tetrachords in Examples 3 and 4 to give other voicings. Be sure that you can sing and identify every chord and that you can determine and number at least the outer interval. A useful exercise is to play the outer voices on the piano and sing the inner voices. Then play the inner voices and sing the outer.

GENERAL QUESTIONS ("Simbolo")

GROUP 1

RHYTHM

1. Which of the following statements describes the metric structure of this piece?
   a. Meter is not perceivable.
   b. The meter is constant and unchanging.
   c. There are meter changes.

2. Irregular divisions of the basic pulse (are)(are not) present.

3. The point of greatest rhythmic density (more notes per unit of time) is nearer which part of the piece?

   a. the beginning   b. the middle   c. the end

PITCH

1. The opening interval of the piece is a

   a. major seventh   c. major ninth
   b. minor ninth   d. minor seventh

2. Which of the following does *not* represent an intervallic version of the melodic motive appearing in the piece?

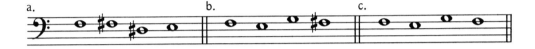

TEXTURE

1. The texture of the piece is essentially

   a. contrapuntal   b. chordal   c. melody and accompaniment

2. Textural variety within the piece is achieved in part by which of the following?

   a. doubling the melodic motive at the octave
   b. changing the position of the melodic motive relative to the accompaniment
   c. dramatic changes in dynamic level accompanying the presentations of the melodic motive

FORM

1. The overall formal structure of the piece is

   a. two-part   b. three-part   c. four-part

2. Which of the following statements is/are true?

   a. Unity is achieved by the general consistency of the number of tones in each melodic unit.
   b. Unity is achieved by the use of ostinato.
   c. Variety is achieved by meter changes and irregular beat divisions.

GROUP 2

RHYTHM

Which of the following help(s) to delineate the sections of the piece?

   a. tempo change
   b. syncopation
   c. change in rhythmic texture
   d. the use of several discrete rhythmic motives
   e. gradual diminution of durational values

PITCH

1. In this piece, antecedent-consequent phrases (do)(do not) occur.

2. Melodic variation within the piece is achieved by

   a. varying the durations of the tones of the motive
   b. adding tones to the motive
   c. playing the motive backwards

3. There (are)(are no) implications of tonality within the piece.

TEXTURE

1. Which of the following help(s) to delineate the sections of the piece?

   a. simultaneous use of staccato and legato articulations
   b. chordal passages alternating with melody-accompaniment texture
   c. changes from forte to piano dynamic levels

2. The basic registral plan of the piece is

   a. low to medium to high
   b. medium to high to low
   c. low to medium to low

FORM

On the diagram below, place the letter of each of the following items in its appropriate location(s).

   a. the melodic motive in retrograde
   b. the beginning of a faster portion marking a main section
   c. the beginning of the third section of the piece
   d. the return of the opening materials

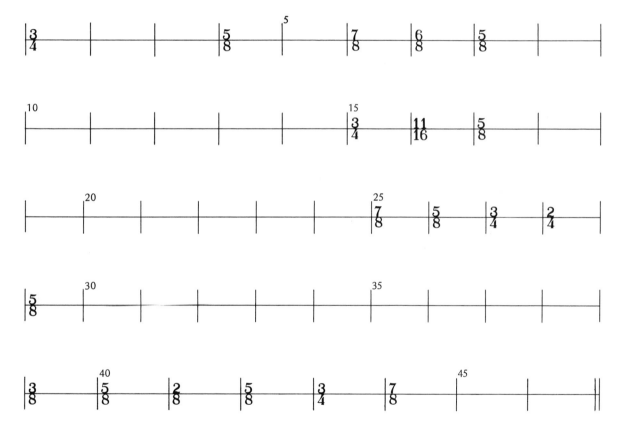

GROUP 3

SCORE STUDY AND DISCUSSION

1. Study the structure of each of the first two sections (measures 1-16 and measures 17-37). Are there relationships between the two sections? Between the two sections and the structure of the piece as a whole?

2. Study thoroughly the rhythmic structure of the piece. How do meter changes and irregular beat divisions contribute to the ongoing nature of the piece?

3. What forms of the twelve-tone set are used in "Simbolo"? Is there a relationship between the twelve-tone set and the phrase structure? (Hint: Are the phrases twelve tones long?)

PRACTICE DRILLS ("Simbolo")

RHYTHM

Tap or intone each of the following rhythmic patterns. Then play them on your instrument, being sure to give all notes their full value. (Perform two-line patterns either with another student or at the piano, playing one line while tapping or intoning the other, then reversing the procedure.)

1. (mm. 15-17)

2. (mm. 6-8)

3. (mm. 25-29)

4. (mm. 38-41)

5. (mm. 42-45)

6. (mm. 15-16)

7. (mm. 37-41)

8. (mm. 6-8)

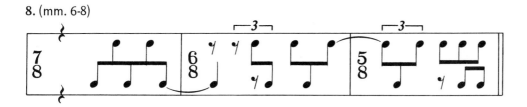

PITCH PATTERNS

Sing each of the following nonrhythmicized pitch-pattern excerpts, transposing up or down an octave as necessary to accommodate your voice range. Then play them on your instrument to check your accuracy. As in the first, indicate in semitone notation the interval between each pair of pitches.

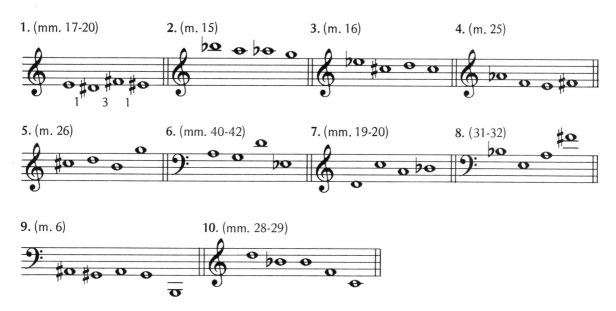

DIAD PATTERNS

Sing the following diad patterns from the bottom tone up and from the top tone down. As in the first, indicate in semitone notation the interval of each diad.

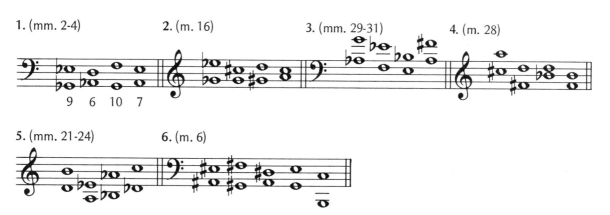

TRICHORDS

Sing the following trichords from the bottom tone up and from the top tone down.
As in the first, indicate in semitone notation the intervals of each trichord.

1. (m. 42) 2. (m. 15) 3. (m. 28) 4. (m. 5)   5. (m. 25) 6. (m. 27) 7. (m. 33) 8. (m. 20) 9. (m. 10)

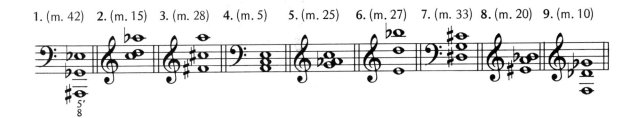

TETRACHORDS

Sing the following tetrachords from the bottom tone up and from the top tone
down. As in the first, indicate in semitone notation the intervals of each tetrachord.

1. (m. 2)   2. (m. 34)   3. (m. 11)   4. (m. 7)   5. (m. 15)

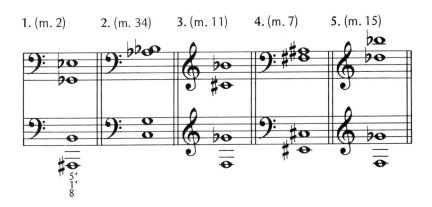

DICTATION AND ANALYSIS ("Simbolo")

PITCH PATTERNS

DRILL 1   You will hear ten pitch patterns, each consisting of either four or five pitches. As in the first, indicate in semitone notation the distance (span) between the first and last pitches of each pattern. The suggested number of hearings is two

1. _1_   2. ____   3. ____   4. ____   5. ____

6. ____   7. ____   8. ____   9. ____   10. ____

DRILL 2   You will hear the same ten patterns again. The first pitch of each pattern has been supplied. Complete the notation and indicate in semitone notation the interval between each pair of pitches. The suggested number of hearings for each pattern is given in parentheses.

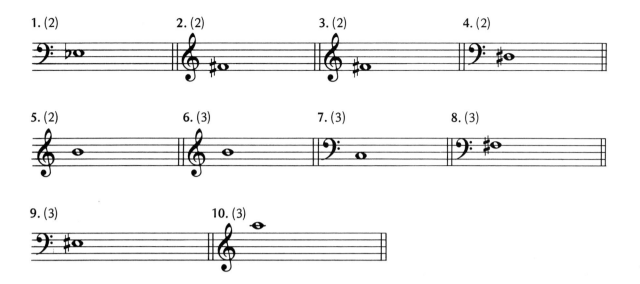

DIAD PATTERNS

DRILL 1   You will hear six diad patterns, each consisting of four diads. As in the first, indicate in semitone notation the interval of each diad. The suggested number of hearings is three.

1. 10-6-10-7   2. _____   3. _____

4. _____   5. _____   6. _____

DRILL 2   You will hear the same six patterns again. The first diad in each pattern has been supplied. Notate the remaining diads. The suggested number of hearings is three.

TRICHORDS

You are given the highest (stem up) or the lowest (stem down) pitch in each trichord. As in the first, notate the remaining pitches and indicate in semitone notation the intervals of each trichord. The suggested number of hearings is three.

TETRACHORDS

You are given the highest (stem up) or the lowest (stem down) pair of pitches in each tetrachord. As in the first, notate the remaining pitches and indicate in semitone notation the intervals of each tetrachord. The suggested number of hearings is three.

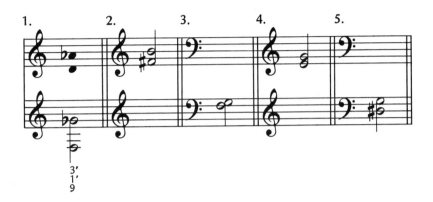

MELODIES

IN ONE VOICE   Complete each of the following melodic excerpts. The basic pulse (or a simple subdivision of the pulse) is given below each. The suggested number of hearings is three.

Complete the voices of the following excerpts as indicated above each. The suggested number of hearings is given in parentheses.

1. Complete all three voices (3)

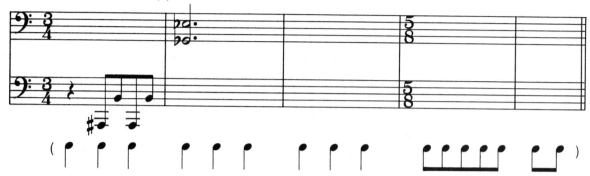

2. Complete outer voices (3)

3. Complete both voices (4)

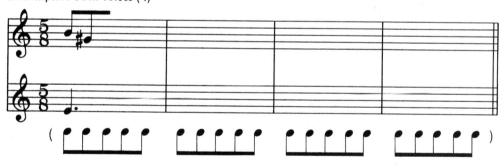

4. Complete outer voices (4)

GENERAL QUESTIONS ("Fregi")

GROUP 1

RHYTHM

1. Meter (is)(is not) generally perceivable in this piece.

2. Cadences in the melodic line are created by

   a. rests   b. longer notes   c. changes in tempo

3. Contributing to the flow of the melody in each half of the piece is/are

   a. a systematic diminution of note values
   b. a general nonagreement in the articulation of melodic and accompanimental elements
   c. a variety of durational values accompanying a dramatic pitch contour

PITCH

1. The melodic line is (motivic)(nonmotivic).

2. The melodic line in each half of the piece consists of

   a. two phrases of equal length
   b. one long phrase
   c. two phrases of unequal length

3. The initial melodic interval of each half of the piece is a

   a. perfect fifth   c. major sixth
   b. minor seventh   d. major seventh

4. The accompanying diad at the cadence at the end of each half of the piece is a

   a. perfect fourth   c. perfect fifth
   b. major third   d. major seventh

TEXTURE

1. The texture of the piece is

   a. contrapuntal   b. note-against-note   c. melody and accompaniment

2. After the initial phrase, the texture throughout employs

   a. three voices
   b. three voices with a fourth added at major cadence points
   c. a balance of two, three, and four voices.

3. Which of the following contributes most to the form of the piece?

   a. change of dynamics
   b. contour and wide range of the melody
   c. variety of articulation in the melodic phrases

FORM

1. The basic structure of the piece is (symmetrical)(asymmetrical).

2. Which pair of terms describes the relationship of the two halves of the piece in terms of its twelve-tone details?

   a. prime and prime   b. prime and inversion   c. prime and retrograde

3. Rhythm, pitch, and texture combine to create which of the following plans for each half of the piece?

   a. a gradual increase in intensity culminated by the cadence
   b. a build-up of intensity in the first phrase followed by a decrease in the second
   c. a build-up of intensity to the midpoint of the second phrase followed by a decrease to the cadence

GROUP 2

1. Study the rhythm of this piece. How does the composer avoid a feeling of meter? How is a sense of rhythmic climax reached in each phrase? How does the piece achieve a sense of cadence in each half? Why is the ending felt to be an ending?

2. How is the twelve-tone set handled in this piece? Do phrases coincide with forms of the set? How is "Fregi" different from "Simbolo" in the handling of the set and its subsets? How are the two alike in this regard?

PRACTICE DRILLS ("Fregi")

RHYTHM

Tap or intone each of the following rhythmic patterns. Then play them on your instrument, being sure to give all notes their full value. (Perform two-line patterns either with another student or at the piano, playing one line while tapping or intoning the other, then reversing the procedure.)

1. (mm. 1-6)

2. (mm. 6-10)

3. (mm. 3-6)

4. (mm. 6-8)

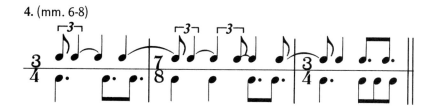

PITCH PATTERNS

Sing each of the following nonrhythmicized pitch-pattern excerpts, transposing up or down an octave as necessary to accommodate your voice range. Then play them on your instrument to check for accuracy. As in the first, indicate in semitone notation the interval between each pair of pitches.

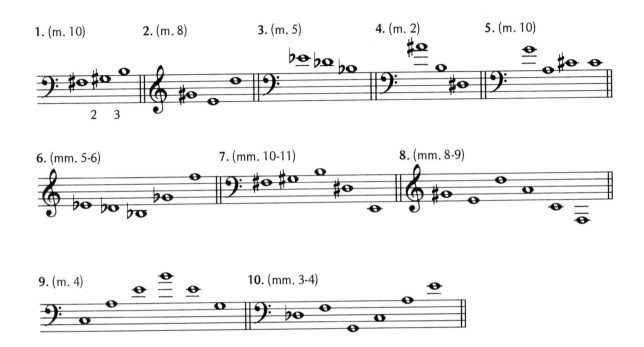

DIAD PATTERNS

Sing the following diad patterns from the bottom tone up and from the top tone down. As in the first, indicate in semitone notation the interval of each diad.

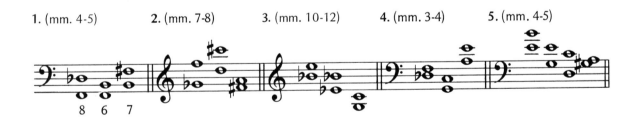

TRICHORDS

Sing the following trichords from the bottom tone up and from the top tone down. As in the first, indicate in semitone notation the intervals of each trichord.

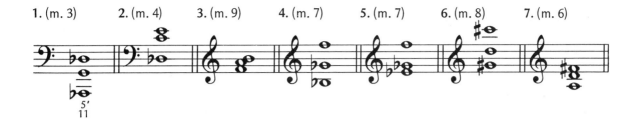

TETRACHORDS

Sing the following tetrachords from the bottom tone up and from the top tone down. As in the first, indicate in semitone notation the intervals of each tetrachord.

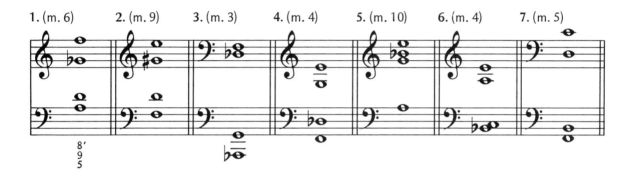

DICTATION AND ANALYSIS ("Fregi")

PITCH PATTERNS

DRILL 1   You will hear ten pitch patterns, each consisting of three to seven tones. As in the first, indicate in semitone notation the distance (span) between the first and last pitches of each pattern. The suggested number of hearings is two.

1. _4_   2. ___   3. ___   4. ___   5. ___

6. ___   7. ___   8. ___   9. ___   10. ___

DRILL 2   You will hear the same ten patterns again. The first pitch of each pattern has been supplied. Complete the notation and indicate in semitone notation the interval between each pair of pitches. The suggested number of hearings for each pattern is given in parentheses.

1. (2)   2. (2)   3. (2)   4. (2)   5. (2)

DIAD PATTERNS

DRILL 1   You will hear six diad patterns, each consisting of three diads. As in the first, indicate in semitone notation the interval of each diad. The suggested number of hearings is three.

1. 11-3-2   2. _____   3. _____

4. _____   5. _____   6. _____

DRILL 2   You will hear the same six patterns again. The first diad in each pattern has been supplied. Notate the remaining diads. The suggested number of hearings is three.

TRICHORDS

You are given the highest (stem up) or the lowest (stem down) pitch in each trichord. As in the first, notate the remaining pitches and indicate in semitone notation the intervals of each trichord. The suggested number of hearings is three.

TETRACHORDS

You are given the highest (stem up) or the lowest (stem down) pair of pitches in each tetrachord. As in the first, notate the remaining pitches and indicate in semitone notation the intervals of each tetrachord. The suggested number of hearings is three.

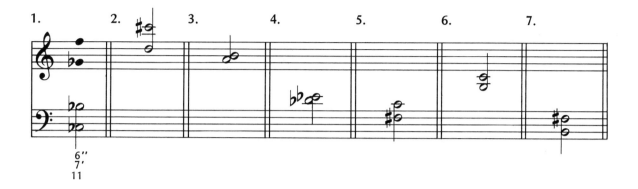

MELODIES

Complete each of the following one-voice melodic excerpts. The basic pulse (or a simple subdivision of the pulse) is given below each excerpt to help orient you. The suggested number of hearings is four.

ANSWERS

UNIT 1 (Dunstable)

GENERAL QUESTIONS

GROUP 1	GROUP 2	GROUP 3
Rhythm: 1. faster 2. c	Rhythm: 1. b 2. c	Rhythm: 1. c 2. b
Pitch: 1. c 2. does	Pitch: 1. c 2. d 3. d	Pitch: 1. a 2. a, c 3. a, b, c, d, e
Texture: 1. b 2. frequently	Texture: 1. b 2. a	Texture: 1. b 2. d
Form: 1. c 2. does	Form: c	Form: a. (7) d. (7) g. (1)
		b. (2) e. (5) h. (4)
		c. (7) f. (3) i. (6)

DICTATION AND ANALYSIS

RHYTHM

1. (mm. 27-29)

2. (mm. 50-54)

3. (mm. 7-9)

4. (mm. 55-58)

5. (mm. 39-42)

PITCH PATTERNS

1. (mm. 19-20)   2. (mm. 23-24)   3. (mm. 20-22)   4. (mm. 46-49)

5. (mm. 35-38)   6. (mm. 26-29)

MELODIES

1. (mm. 19-22)

2. (mm. 1-9)

3. (mm. 10-15)

4. (mm. 10-18)

5. (mm. 31-38)

COUNTERPOINT

1. (mm. 43-45)

2. (mm. 23-26)

**SONORITY
TYPES**

1. (m. 4) 2. (m. 6) 3. (m. 8) 4. (m. 12) 5. (m. 13) 6. (m. 15) 7. (m. 27) 8. (m. 32)

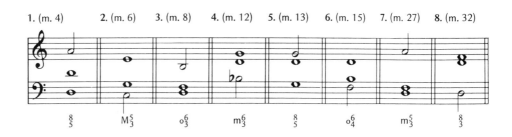

**SELECTIVE
LISTENING**

Nonchord
tones

1. (mm. 19-22)

2. (mm. 1-3)

3. (mm. 51-54)

4. (mm. 39-42)

Tonal change

1. (mm. 46-54)

2. (mm. 31-38)

Cadence types

1. (mm. 19-22)

2. (mm. 39-42)

HARMONIC PROGRESSIONS

1. (mm. 12-15)

X (X) X   X   X   (X) X   X X

2. (mm. 35-38)

X   X

3. (mm. 16-18)

X   X

UNIT 2 (Josquin)

GENERAL QUESTIONS

GROUP 1	GROUP 2	GROUP 3
Rhythm: 1. does 2. c	Rhythm: 1. a 2. d 3. b	Rhythm: 1. b 2. a
Pitch: 1. b 2. c	Pitch: 1. b 2. d	Pitch: 1. b 2. a 3. d 4. b
Texture: 1. c 2. c	Texture: 1. duet 2. c	Texture: 1. d 2. does
Form: 1. a 2. important	Form: 1. b 2. a, b, c, d, e	Form: a. (5) d. (6) g. (4) j. (5)
		b. (6) e. (1) h. (7)
		c. (2) f. (3) i. (4)

DICTATION AND ANALYSIS

RHYTHM

1. (mm. 14-17)

2. (mm. 61-66)

3. (mm. 1-5)

PITCH
PATTERNS

1. (mm. 2-3)   2. (mm. 36-37)   3. (mm. 38-39)   4. (mm. 35-36)

5. (mm. 30-32)   6. (mm. 74-75)

MELODIES

1. (mm. 99-102)

A

B

2. (mm. 103-107)

A

B

3. (mm. 18-21)

A

B

4. (mm. 87-92)

5. (mm. 30-34)

COUNTERPOINT

1. (mm. 32-34)

2. (mm. 5-7)

3. (mm. 21-23)

**SONORITY
TYPES**

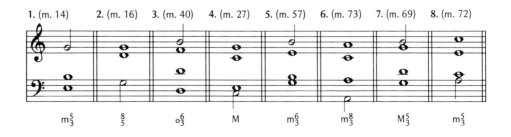

1. (m. 14) 2. (m. 16) 3. (m. 40) 4. (m. 27) 5. (m. 57) 6. (m. 73) 7. (m. 69) 8. (m. 72)

m_3^5 $\frac{8}{5}$ o_3^6 M m_3^6 m_3^8 M_3^5 m_3^5

**SELECTIVE
LISTENING**

**Nonchord
tones**

1. (mm. 34-35)

2. (mm. 30-32)

3. (mm. 20-23)

4. (mm. 27-30)

5. (mm. 92-94)

6. (mm. 67-73)

**Tonal
change**

1. (mm. 20-23)

C major   G major

2. (mm. 67-73)

C major   A minor

3. (mm. 1-5)

A minor   C major

Parallel intervals

1. (mm. 99-103)

d.

2. (mm. 80-84)

b.

HARMONIC PROGRESSIONS

1. (mm. 56-60)

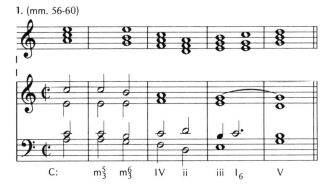

C: m⁵₃   m⁶₃   IV   ii   iii   I₆   V

2. (mm. 27-29)

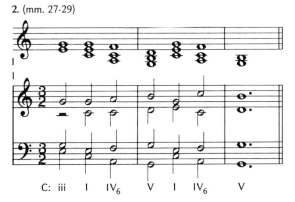

C: iii   I   IV₆   V   I   IV₆   V

3. (mm. 42-44)

UNIT 3 (Gesualdo)

GENERAL QUESTIONS

GROUP 1

Rhythm: 1. duple 2. b
Pitch: 1. c 2. c 3. major
Texture: 1. c 2. d
Form: 1. a 2. different

GROUP 2

Rhythm: 1. c 2. c
Pitch: 1. a 2. d
Texture: 1. imitative
        2. contrapuntal
Form: 1. A different
      2. c

GROUP 3

Rhythm: 1. d 2. c
Pitch: 1. b 2. c 3. c
Texture: 1. c 2. contrapuntal
        3. b
Form: a. (2) c. (5) e. (3)
      b. (4) d. (6) f. (1)

DICTATION AND ANALYSIS

RHYTHM

1. (mm. 15-17)

2. (mm. 28-31)

3. (mm. 38-42)

4. (mm. 9-11)

PITCH PATTERNS

1. (mm. 6-8) **2.** (mm. 43-44) **3.** (mm. 8-9) **4.** (mm. 1-3)

5. (mm. 10-11) **6.** (mm. 44-45) **7.** (mm. 15-16)

8. (mm. 23-25) **9.** (mm. 40-42) **10.** (mm. 8-11)

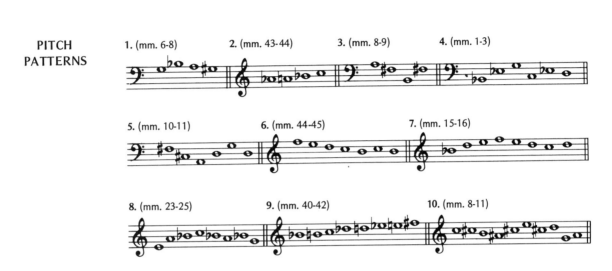

MELODIES

1. (mm. 9-11)

A

B

2. (mm. 1-4)

A

B

3. (mm. 12-15)

A

B

4. (mm. 26-31)

COUNTERPOINT   **1.** (mm. 44-45)

2. (mm. 23-25)

3. (mm. 34-36)

4. (mm. 18-23)

5. (mm. 27-31)

SONORITY TYPES

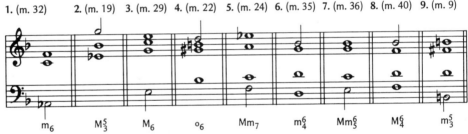

1. (m. 32)   2. (m. 19)   3. (m. 29)   4. (m. 22)   5. (m. 24)   6. (m. 35)   7. (m. 36)   8. (m. 40)   9. (m. 9)

m_6 M_3^5 M_6 $^o6$ Mm_7 m_4^6 Mm_5^6 M_4^6 m_3^5

SELECTIVE LISTENING

Nonchord tones

1. (mm. 12-13)

2. (mm. 30-31)

3. (mm. 20-23)

Tonal change

(mm. 18-23)

B♭ major   A major

Parallel intervals

1. (mm. 15-16)

2. (mm. 16-18)

3. (mm. 29-31)

4. (mm. 35-36)

Cadence types

(mm. 1-4)

g: iv₆   V   d: iv₆   V

d.   d.

1 (a). (mm. 44-45)

1 (b). (mm. 7-10)

2 (a). (m. 11)

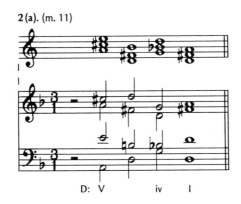

2 (b). (mm. 24-26)

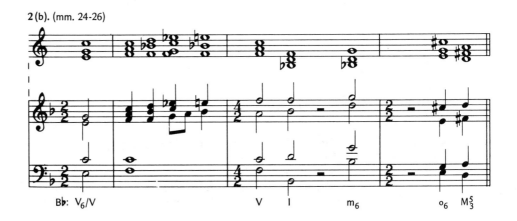

UNIT 4 (Purcell)

GENERAL QUESTIONS

GROUP 1

Rhythm: 1. simple   2. four
           3. dotted rhythms
Pitch: 1. fourth   2. d   3. b
Texture: b
Form: 1. b   2. b

GROUP 2

Rhythm: 1. c   2. c
Pitch: 1. d.   2. d   3. does
Texture: c
Form: 1. a   2. c

GROUP 3

Rhythm: 1. a   2. Not all
Pitch: 1. a, c, d   2. relative
Texture: a, c, d
Form: (below)

DICTATION AND ANALYSIS

RHYTHM

1. (mm. 18-20)

2. (mm. 13-15)

3. (mm. 21-25)

PITCH PATTERNS

1. (mm. 19-20)　　　　　　**2.** (mm. 24-25)

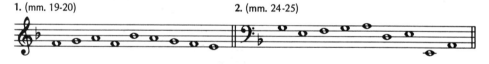

3. (mm. 41-45)　　　　　　**4.** (mm. 20-23)

MELODIES

1. (mm. 5-8)

2. (mm. 1-5)

3. (mm. 27-23)

COUNTERPOINT

1. (mm. 45-49)

2. (mm. 41-45)

SONORITY TYPES

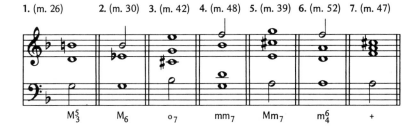

M_3^5 M_6 $^o7$ mm_7 Mm_7 m_4^6 +

SELECTIVE LISTENING

Nonchord tones

Tonal change

D minor

F major

HARMONIC PROGRESSIONS

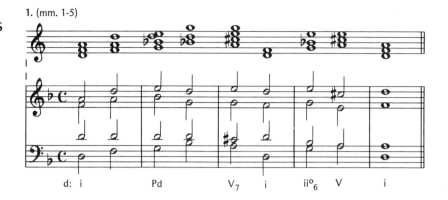

1. (mm. 1-5)

d: i   Pd   V₇ i   ii°₆ V   i

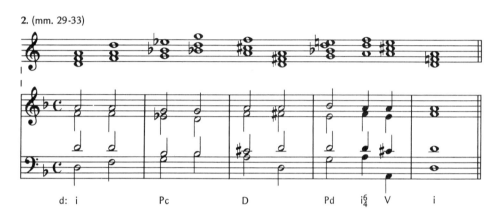

2. (mm. 29-33)

d: i   Pc   D   Pd   i⁶₄ V   i

UNIT 5 (Bach)

GENERAL QUESTIONS

GROUP 1

Rhythm: 1. b 2. does not 3. a
Pitch: 1. c 2. b
Texture: 1. b 2. b
Form: b, c

GROUP 2

Rhythm: 1. b 2. b
Pitch: 1. c 2. d
Texture: a
Form: 1. a, b 2. a, b, c, d

GROUP 3

Rhythm: 1. a 2. a, b, d
Pitch: 1. b 2. a, c
Texture and Form: (below)

1.

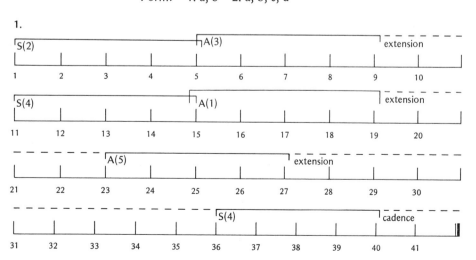

DICTATION AND ANALYSIS

RHYTHM

1. (mm. 127-29)

2. (mm. 13-17)

3. (mm. 203-05)

4. (mm. 19-23)

5. (mm. 37-41)

PITCH PATTERNS

1. (mm. 1-3)

2. (mm. 5-7)

3. (mm. 19-20)

4. (mm. 63-65)

5. (mm. 103-05)

6. (mm. 131-33)

7. (mm. 52-53)

MELODIES

COUNTERPOINT

2. (mm. 63-67)

3. (mm. 179-83)

4. (mm. 159-63)

5. (mm. 171-75)

SONORITY TYPES

1. (m. 213)   2. (m. 243)   3. (m. 72)   4. (m. 60)   5. (m. 23)   6. (m. 86)   7. (m. 144)   8. (m. 99)   9. (m. 234)

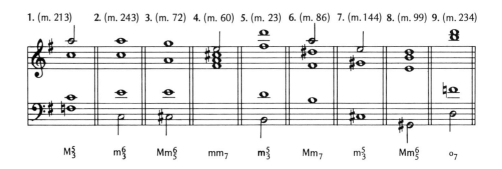

M_3^5 m_3^6 Mm_5^6 mm_7 $\mathbf{m_3^5}$ Mm_7 m_3^5 Mm_5^6 $°_7$

SELECTIVE LISTENING

Nonchord tones

1. (mm. 85-87)

2. (mm. 15-17)

3. (mm. 39-41)

4. (mm. 68-71)

e.   e.   b.

Tonal change

1. (mm. 87-95)

E minor

D major

2. (mm. 79-87)

G major

E minor

HARMONIC PROGRESSIONS

1. (mm. 131-33)

b: iv₆   VI   ii∅⁶₅   V₇   i

2. (mm. 38-41)

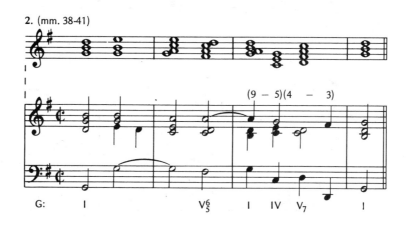

(9 — 5)(4 — 3)

G: I   V⁶₅   I   IV   V₇   I

3. (mm. 159-63)

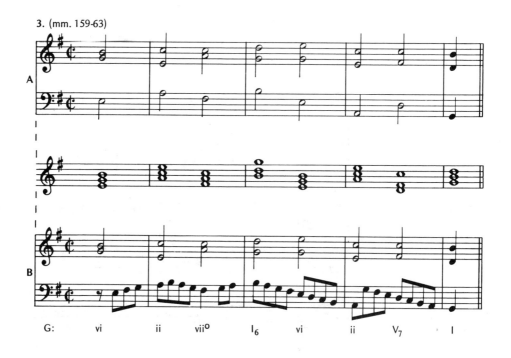

A

B

G: vi   ii   viiº   I₆   vi   ii   V₇   I

4. (mm. 101-05)

A

B

G: ii   vi   IV V₆   V I

5. (mm. 229-36)

A

B

G: I   V

A

B

IV   ii   V ii₆ V   I

UNIT 6 (Haydn)

GENERAL QUESTIONS

GROUP 1	GROUP 2	GROUP 3
Rhythm: 1. b 2. c 3. does not	Rhythm: 1. c 2. a	Rhythm: 1. b 2. a, b
Pitch: 1. are 2. c 3. are not	Pitch: 1. c 2. c	Pitch: 1. b 2. b
Texture: 1. b 2. b 3. is	Texture: 1. b, c 2. a 3. a, b, c	Texture: a, c
Form: 1. three 2. c	Form: 1. c 2. a, b, d	Form: (below)

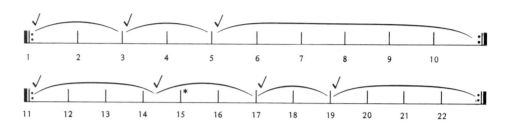

DICTATION AND ANALYSIS

RHYTHM

1. (mm. 42-43)

2. (mm. 14-16)

3. (mm. 54-55)

4. (mm. 27-30)

5. (mm. 40-41)

PITCH PATTERNS

1. (mm. 3-4)   2. (mm. 32-35)   3. (mm. 27-30)

4. (mm. 7-10)   5. (mm. 9-10)

6. (mm. 5-8)

MELODIES

1. (mm. 1-10)

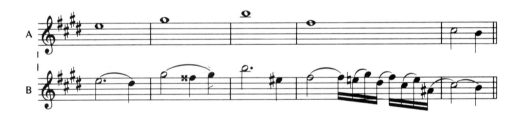

2. (mm. 23-30)

3. (mm. 54-59)

**SONORITY
TYPES**

**SELECTIVE
LISTENING**

**Nonchord
tones**

1. (mm. 11-13)

2. (mm. 31-34)

Tonal change

1. (mm. 5-10)

E major   B major

2. (mm. 31-37)

C major

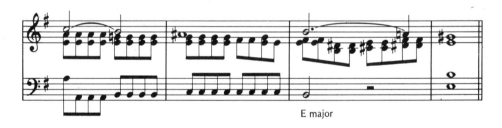

E major

HARMONIC PROGRESSIONS

1. (mm. 1-5)

E: I   V$_2^4$ I$_6$ V$_5^6$ I   V$_2^4$ I$_6$ vii$^{ø}_7$ I

2. (mm. 27-30)

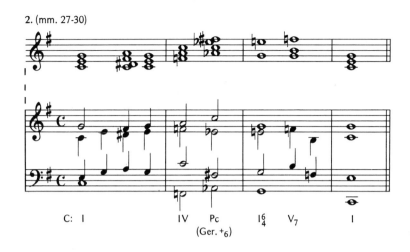

C: I   IV Pc I^6_4 V_7 I
                  (Ger. $+_6$)

3. (mm. 31-34)

C: V_7/ii ii V_7 I

4. (mm. 11-14)

                                Pc
E: V_6/vi vi (V^6_5/V) V^4_2 I_6 V^4_3 I   V

UNIT 7 (Mozart)

GENERAL QUESTIONS

GROUP 1

Rhythm: 1. b   2. simple   3. does not
Pitch: 1. tonic   3. disjunct
       2. c   4. are
Texture: 1. c   2. end
Form: 1. b†   2. c††

GROUP 2

Rhythm: 1. a, b, c
            2. a, b, c
Pitch: 1. b, c   2. a
Texture: 1. c   2. b
Form: 1. d   2. b

GROUP 3

Rhythm: b
Pitch: 1. a, b, c   2. a, b   3. d
Texture: 1. a   2. a, c
Form: 1. a, b, c, d   2. a, c

DICTATION AND ANALYSIS

RHYTHM

1. (mm. 13-18)

2. (mm. 195-201)

3. (mm. 26-29)

4. (mm. 56-60)

†(This answer will be *c* if the recorded performance heard includes a repeat of the first main section.)

††(This answer is based on a *b* answer to the preceding question.)

PITCH PATTERNS

1. (m. 30) 2. (m. 8) 3. (mm. 38-39) 4. (mm. 1-3)

5. (m. 198) 6. (mm. 195-96) 7. (mm. 42-46)

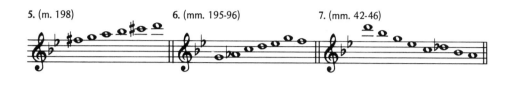

8. (mm. 113-14) 9. (mm. 153-54)

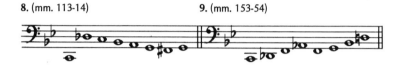

MELODIES

1. (mm. 209-11)

A

B

2. (mm. 30-33)

A

B

3. (mm. 46-49)

A

B

4. (mm. 1-4)

A

B

COUNTERPOINT

1. (mm. 27-30)

2. (mm. 68-72)

3. (mm. 151-54)

4. (mm. 20-24)

5. (mm. 13-16)

SONORITY TYPES

1. (m. 28)   2. (m. 14)   3. (m. 63)   4. (m. 35)   5. (m. 94)   6. (m. 156)   7. (m. 196)   8. (m. 110)   9. (m. 113)

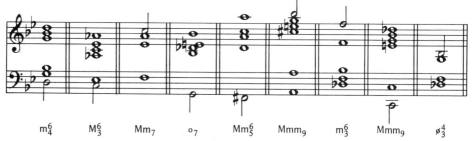

m_4^6 M_3^6 Mm_7 ${}^{\circ}7$ Mm_5^6 Mmm_9 m_3^6 Mmm_9 $ø_3^4$

SELECTIVE LISTENING

Nonchord tones

1. (mm. 9-10)

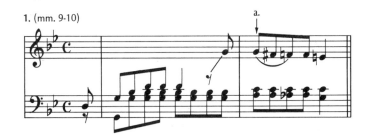

2. (mm. 60-64)

Tonal change

1. (mm. 30-37)

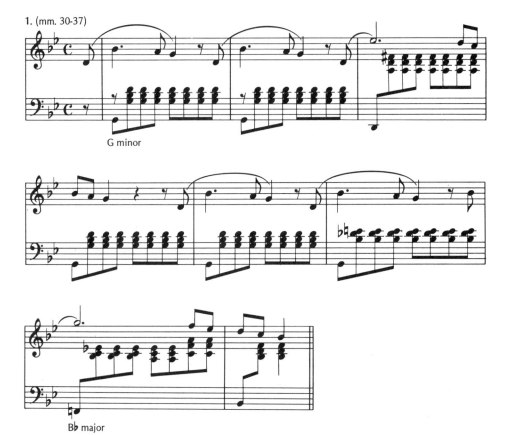

2. (mm. 168-75)

G minor

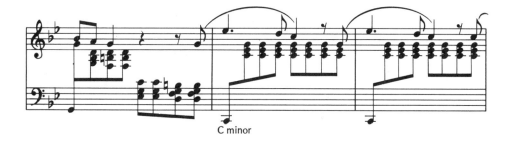

C minor

3. (mm. 101-07)

D♭ major

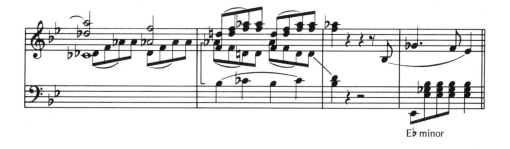

E♭ minor

Harmonic function

1. (mm. 225-28)

g: i   IV₆   Pc   i$^6_4$ V₇   i
                                       (It. +₆)

2. (mm. 20-24)

g: i   Pc   i$^6_4$ V₇   i
                                              (N₆)

HARMONIC PROGRESSIONS

1. (mm. 225-28)

g: i   V₆ — 7   Pc   V
                                                (vii°₇/V)

2. (mm. 24-29)†

A

B

g: i   ♭VI   Pc   i$^6_4$ V   i
                                          (vii°₇/V)

†In this excerpt, each half-note value is equivalent to one measure of the passage in the score.

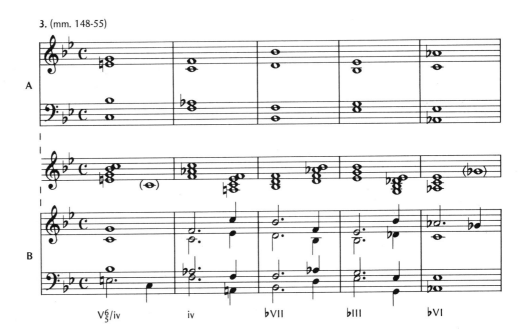

3. (mm. 148-55)

V$^6_5$/iv   iv   ♭VII   ♭III   ♭VI

ii°   iv   V$_8$ — $_7$ i

UNIT 8 (Beethoven)

GENERAL QUESTIONS

GROUP 1

Rhythm: 1. duple 3. is
         2. two
Pitch: 1. d 2. b 3. the same
Texture: 1. chordal 2. b
Form: 1. a 2. b

GROUP 2

Rhythm: 1. b 2. c
Pitch: 1. b 2. does 3. is not
Texture: 1. b 2. a
Form: 1. the same 3. b
       2. different

GROUP 3

Rhythm: 1. a 2. c 3. a
Pitch: 1. a 2. mode
Texture: 1. c 2. is
Form: 1. b 3. a
      2. b 4. abbreviated

DICTATION AND ANALYSIS

RHYTHM

1. (mm. 174-81)

2. (mm. 27-34)

3. (mm. 190-95)

4. (mm. 123-30)

PITCH PATTERNS

1. (m. 51) **2.** (m. 84) **3.** (m. 97-98) **4.** (m. 110)

5. (mm. 114-15) **6.** (mm. 113-14)

MELODIES

1. (mm. 27-34)

A

B

2. (mm. 35-42)

A

B

3. (mm. 218-21)

4. (mm. 51-58)

5. (mm. 101-09)

COUNTERPOINT   **1.** (mm. 162-65)

2. (mm. 187-91)

SONORITY TYPES

1. (m. 4)   2. (m. 10)   3. (m. 7)   4. (m. 131)   5. (m. 132)   6. (m. 136)   7. (m. 219)

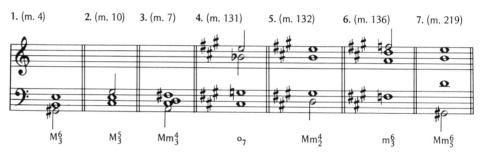

M_3^6 M_3^5 Mm_3^4 $°7$ Mm_2^4 m_3^6 Mm_5^6

SELECTIVE LISTENING

Nonchord tones

1. (mm. 150-53)

2. (mm. 158-61)

Tonal change

1. (mm. 3-10)

A minor   C major

2. (mm. 129-38)

A major   C major

Chord mutation   (mm. 11-18)

Harmonic function   **1. (mm. 101-16)**

Tonic pedal begins

Subdominant   Dominant

2. (mm. 241-50)

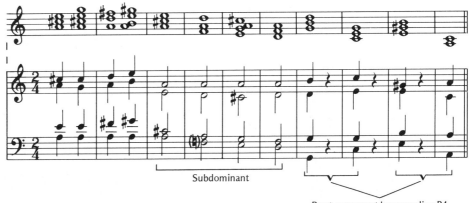

Subdominant

Root movement by ascending P4

(mm. 129-38)

A: I$^6_4$ V   I   °$_7$ Mm$^4_2$ C: I$^6_4$ V$_7$ I

UNIT 9 (Chopin)

GENERAL QUESTIONS

GROUP 1

Rhythm: 1. does   2. twice
Pitch: 1. b   2. b and c
Texture: 1. b
        2. broken chords
        3. different from
Form: 1. important   2. d

GROUP 2

Rhythm: 1. a
        2. triple; duple
        3. last
Pitch: 1. dominant
        2. d
        3. contrasting
Texture: c
Form: 1. varied   2. a

GROUP 3

Rhythm: 1. c   2. c
Pitch: 1. a
        2. fifth
        3. major
Texture: a, b, c, d, and e
Form: (below)

A   B   A'   Coda
1————28 29————56 57—72 73—88 89—100 101—108 109—119
  a   a   b   b   b   a   a'

DICTATION AND ANALYSIS

RHYTHM   1. (mm. 5-7)

2. (mm. 73-80)

5. (mm. 109-13)

6. (mm. 105-09)

COUNTERPOINT

1. (mm. 7-11)

2. (mm. 3-5)

3. (mm. 19-23)

†Parallel octaves are avoided in the actual passage.

SONORITY
TYPES

SELECTIVE
LISTENING

Nonchord
tones

Tonal
change

2. (mm. 63-73)

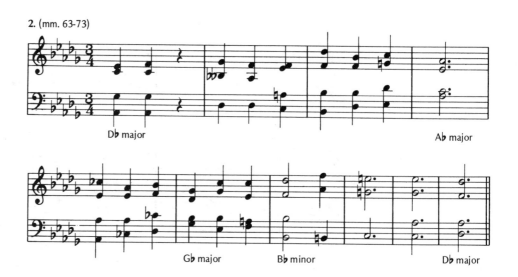

Db major   Ab major

Gb major   Bb minor   Db major

Dominant thirteenth chords

(mm. 63-73)

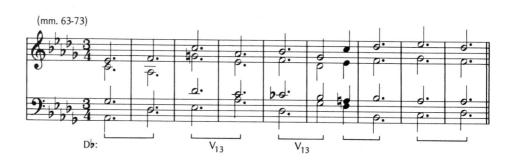

Db: V₁₃   V₁₃

Chromatic third relation

(mm. 119-23)

HARMONIC PROGRESSIONS

1. (mm. 57-64)

Db: I   V₄₃   I₆   IV   V₇   iv₄⁶   I

2. (mm. 105-18)

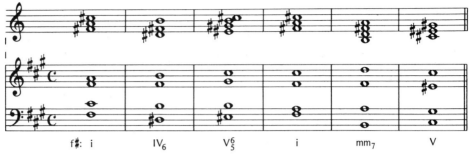

f♯:   i   IV$_6$ V$_5^6$ i   mm$_7$ V

3. (mm. 105-18)

f♯: i   °$_7$ IV$_6$ °$_7$ °$_7$ V$_5^6$

i   mm$_7$ ø$_3^4$ V

4. (mm. 123-27)

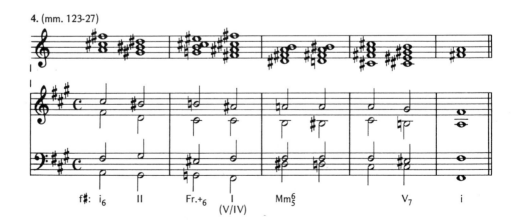

f♯: i$_6$ II   Fr.+$_6$ Mm$_5^6$ V$_7$ i
                       (V/IV)

UNIT 10 (Wolf)

GENERAL QUESTIONS

GROUP 1	GROUP 2	GROUP 3
Rhythm: 1. c 2. compound	Rhythm: 1. a prominent 2. d	Rhythm: 1. b 2. a
Pitch: 1. c 2. a 3. important	Pitch: 1. c 2. tonic	Pitch: a and c
Texture: c	Texture: nonimitative	Texture: b
Form: 1. one 2. is not	Form: 1. d 2. b	Form: a. 13-18 c. 18-21
		b. 7-12

DICTATION AND ANALYSIS

RHYTHM

1. (mm. 17-18)

2. (mm. 7-8)

3. (mm. 14-15)

PITCH PATTERNS

1. (mm. 1-2)   2. (mm. 2-3)   3. (mm. 9-11)   4. (mm. 14-15)

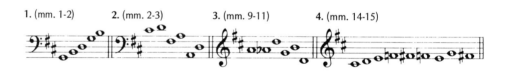

MELODIES

1. (mm. 3-5)

A

B

2. (mm. 5-6)

A

B

3. (mm. 3-4)

4. (mm. 1-3)

5. (mm. 15-16)

6. (mm. 3-6)

COUNTERPOINT   **1.** (mm. 5-6)

2. (mm. 18-21)

SONORITY TYPES

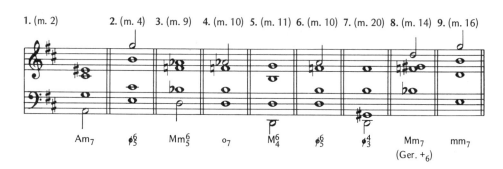

1. (m. 2) **2. (m. 4)** **3. (m. 9)** **4. (m. 10)** **5. (m. 11)** **6. (m. 10)** **7. (m. 20)** **8. (m. 14)** **9. (m. 16)**

Am₇   ø⁶₅   Mm⁶₅   o₇   M⁶₄   ø⁶₅   ø⁴₃   Mm₇   mm₇
(Ger. +₆)

SELECTIVE LISTENING

Nonchord tones

1. (mm. 7-8)

2. (mm. 1-3)

3. (mm. 8-9)

4. (mm. 11-12)

Harmonic
function

(mm. 11-12)

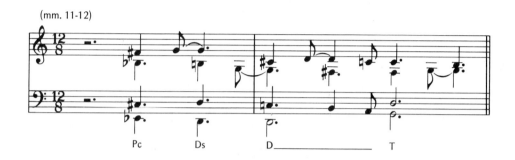

Pc   Ds   D_____ T

HARMONIC
PROGRESSIONS

A. **1.** (mm. 8-9)

F major   B♭ major

2. (mm. 7-8)

D major   F major

B. **1.** (mm. 9-10)

M   ø7   MM$^6_5$ °7   m6

C. 1. (mm. 1-3)

D: viio$_2$ I$^6_4$ mm$^6_5$ ϕ_7 V$_7$ _____ I

2. (mm. 3-6)

D: I   o$_7$ IV$^6_4$ ϕ^6_5 Mm$_7$ I$_6$ IV   V$^4_2$ I$_6$ I V

UNIT 11 (Debussy)

GENERAL QUESTIONS

GROUP 1	GROUP 2	GROUP 3
Rhythm: 1. c 2. d	Rhythm: 1. a, b 2. c	Rhythm: a, b, d
Pitch: 1. c 2. b 3. a, b	Pitch: 1. d 2. c	Pitch: 1. a, b, d 2. d
Texture: a, b, c, d	Texture: 1. c 2. a	Texture and Form: (below)
Form: b	Form: 1. a, b, d 2. h	

```
        A              B              C              D
 ||                                                        ||
 ||b.          h. d. g.          a.          c.  g.  f.  h.
                  e.             h.
```

(Letters appearing more than once in the diagram indicate alternative responses.)

DICTATION AND ANALYSIS

RHYTHM

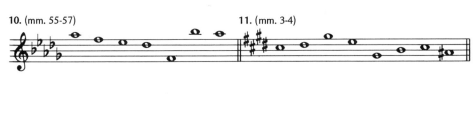

MELODIES

SONORITY TYPES

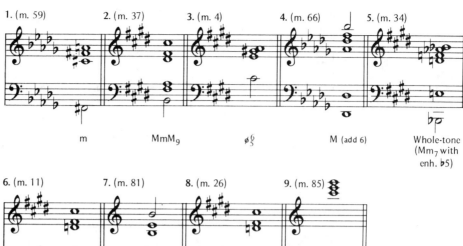

m   MmM$_9$ $\emptyset^6_5$ M (add 6)   Whole-tone (Mm$_7$ with enh. ♭5)

MM$_7$ mm$_7$ (MmM$_9$ (plus 13))   M$^6_3$

SELECTIVE LISTENING

1. (mm. 21-23)

2. (mm. 24-26)

3. (107-08)

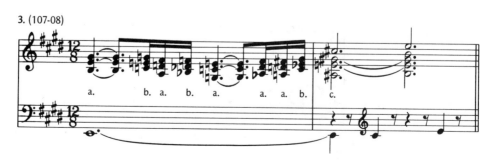

4. (mm. 55-63)

HARMONIC PROGRESSIONS

1. (m. 13)

2. (mm. (mm. 41-43)

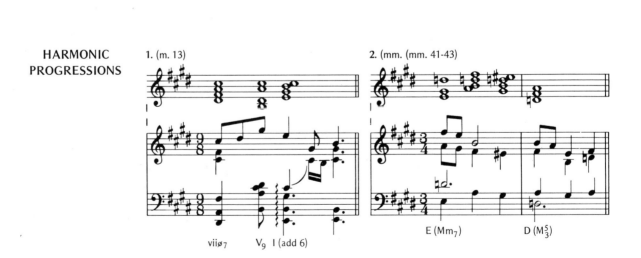

viiø₇   V₉   I (add 6)

E (Mm₇)   D (M⅗)

UNIT 12 (Stravinsky)

GENERAL QUESTIONS

GROUP 1

Rhythm: 1. b 2. a 3. does
Pitch: 1. d 2. does 3. a
Texture: 1. c 2. a 3. does
Form: 1. d 2. different

GROUP 2

Rhythm: 1. b 3. a
         2. c
Pitch: 1. different from
       2. a, c 3. c
Texture: a, c, d, e
Form: 1. b 2. a

GROUP 3

Rhythm: 1. is not 2. a, b
Pitch: 1. b 2. c 3. d
Texture: a, b, d
Form: (page 346)

DICTATION AND ANALYSIS

RHYTHM

1. (mm. 30-32)   **2.** (mm. 28-31)

3. (mm. 73-77)

4. (mm. 13-14)

5. (mm. 36-40)

PITCH PATTERNS

1. (mm. 4-5)   **2.** (mm. 12-14)

3. (mm. 22-26)   4. (m. 1)

5. (m. 52)   6. (mm. 45-47)

MELODIES

1. (mm. 65-68)

A

B

2. (mm. 12-14)

A

B

3. (mm. 70-73)

A

B

4. (mm. 77-81)

A

B

5. (mm. 47-49)

A

B

COUNTERPOINT

1. (mm. 33-35)

2. (mm. 59-61)

3. (mm. 10-11)

4. (m. 42)

5. (mm. 49-50)

6. (mm. 20-21)

SONORITY TYPES

1. (m. 7) 2. (m. 11) 3. (m. 47) 4. (m. 26) 5. (m. 13) 6. (m. 58) 7. (m. 59) 8. (m. 80) 9. (m. 61)

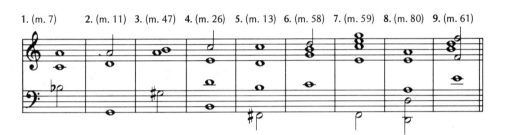

SELECTIVE LISTENING

Nonchord tones

1. (m. 1)

2. (mm. 40-41)

Tonal change

(mm. 37-40)

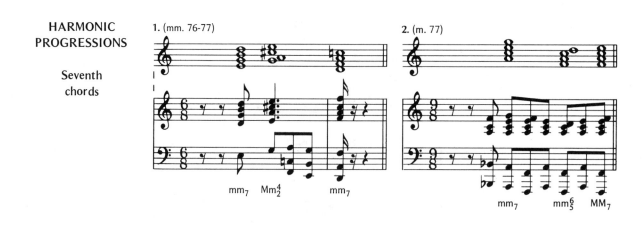

HARMONIC PROGRESSIONS

Seventh chords

1. (mm. 76-77)   mm₇   Mm₂⁴   mm₇

2. (m. 77)   mm₇   mm₅⁶   MM₇

Harmonic function   (mm. 56-58)   T   P   D

UNIT 13 (Bartók)

GENERAL QUESTIONS

GROUP 1	GROUP 2	GROUP 3
Rhythm: 1. do 2. does	Rhythm: 1. b 2. b	Rhythm: 1. b 2. a
Pitch: 1. recurring 2. d	Pitch: 1. d 2. d	Pitch: 1. a 2. does 3. a, c
Texture: 1. b 2. b	Texture: 1. c	Texture: 1. a, b, c, d 2. d
Form: 1. d 2. a	Form: 1. different 2. varied	Form: d, f, h, i, a, g, c, e, b

DICTATION AND ANALYSIS

RHYTHM

1. (mm. 1-3)

2. (mm. 11-12)

3. (m. 38)

4. (mm. 48-51)

5. (mm. 19-21)

PITCH PATTERNS

1. (m. 14)   **2.** (m. 9)   **3.** (m. 25-26)

4. (m. 19)   **5.** (mm. 1-3)

MELODIES

1. (mm. 35-36)

2. (mm. 6-8)

3. (mm. 1-4)

4. (mm. 49-50)

SONORITY TYPES

1. (m. 42) **2.** (m. 40) **3.** (m. 41) **4.** (m. 45) **5.** (m. 47) **6.** (m. 47)

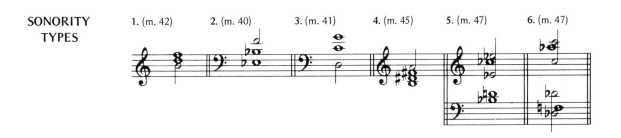

SELECTIVE LISTENING

Intervals

(mm. 46-48)

b.

Sonority types

(mm. 44-45)

Added tone chords

(m. 33)

UNIT 14 (Dallapiccola)

GENERAL QUESTIONS ("Simbolo")

GROUP 1	GROUP 2
Rhythm: 1. c 2. are 3. b	Rhythm: a, b, c
Pitch: 1. b 2. c	Pitch: 1. do 2. a, c 3. are
Texture: 1. c 2. b	Texture: 1. a, b 2. c
Form: 1. b 2. a, b, c	Form: (below)

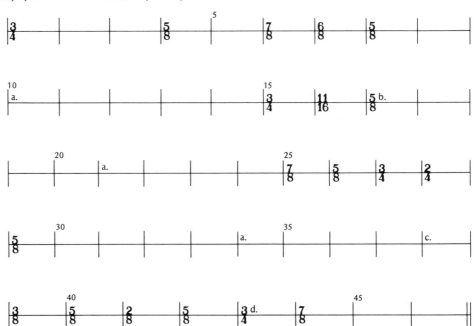

DICTATION AND ANALYSIS

PITCH PATTERNS

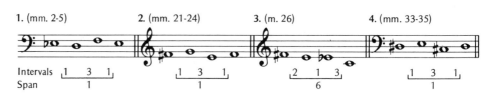

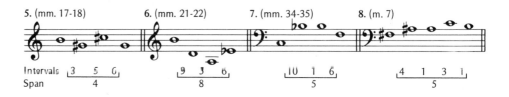

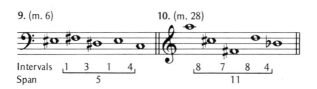

DIAD PATTERNS

1. (mm. 11-14)   2. (mm. 33-36)   3. (mm. 17-20)   4. (m. 15)

10 6 10 7   1 10 6 3   3 6 10 1   9 6 8 8

5. (m. 26)   6. (m. 27)

4 4 6 11   11 6 8 8

TRICHORDS

1. (m. 4) 2. (m. 30) 3. (m. 16) 4. (m. 31) 5. (m. 16) 6. (m. 26) 7. (m. 32) 8. (m. 29) 9. (m. 17)

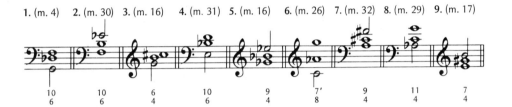

10 10 6 10 9 7' 9 11 7
6   6   4 6   4 8   4 4   4

TETRACHORDS

1. (m. 12)   2. (m. 21)   3. (m. 35)   4. (m. 14)   5. (m. 33)

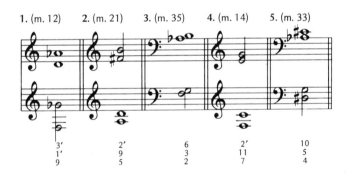

3' 2' 6 2' 10
1' 9   3 11 5
9   5   2 7   4

MELODIES

In one voice

1. (mm. 6-8)

2. (mm. 15-16)

3. (mm. 28-29)

**In two
or more
voices**

1. (mm. 1-5)

staccatissimo

2. (mm. 15-16)

3. (mm. 17-20)

4. (mm. 25-29)

GENERAL QUESTIONS ("Fregi")

GROUP 1

Rhythm: 1. is not 2. a, b 3. b, c
Pitch: 1. nonmotivic 2. c 3. d 4. a
Texture: 1. c 2. b 3. b
Form: 1. symmetrical 2. b 3. a

DICTATION AND ANALYSIS

**PITCH
PATTERNS**

1. (m. 2-3)　　　**2.** (m. 3)　　　**3.** (m. 4)　　　**4.** (m. 9)　　　**5.** (m. 9)

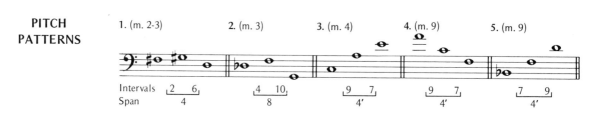

Intervals　⌊2　6⌋　　⌊4　10⌋　　⌊9　7⌋　　⌊9　7⌋　　⌊7　9⌋
Span　　　　　4　　　　　　8　　　　　4'　　　　　4'　　　　　4'

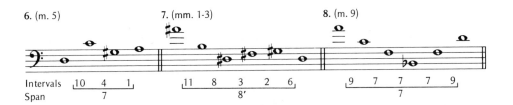

6. (m. 5)   7. (mm. 1-3)   8. (m. 9)

Intervals | 10 4 1 | 11 8 3 2 6 | 9 7 7 7 9
Span | 7 | 8' | 7

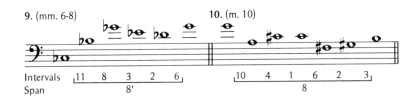

9. (mm. 6-8)   10. (m. 10)

Intervals | 11 8 3 2 6 | 10 4 1 6 2 3
Span | 8' | 8

DIAD PATTERNS

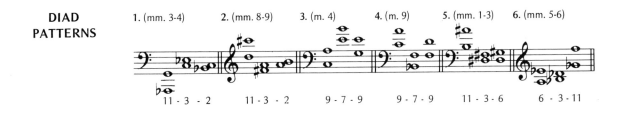

1. (mm. 3-4)   2. (mm. 8-9)   3. (m. 4)   4. (m. 9)   5. (mm. 1-3)   6. (mm. 5-6)

11 - 3 - 2   11 - 3 - 2   9 - 7 - 9   9 - 7 - 9   11 - 3 - 6   6 - 3 - 11

TRICHORDS

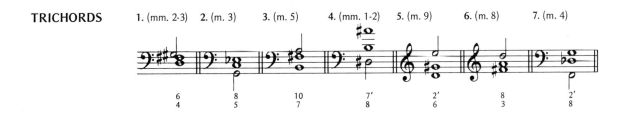

1. (mm. 2-3)   2. (m. 3)   3. (m. 5)   4. (mm. 1-2)   5. (m. 9)   6. (m. 8)   7. (m. 4)

6
4   8
5   10
7   7'
8   2'
6   8
3   2'
8

TETRACHORDS

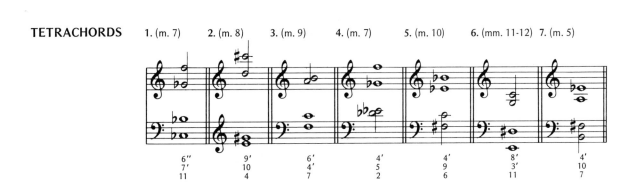

1. (m. 7)   2. (m. 8)   3. (m. 9)   4. (m. 7)   5. (m. 10)   6. (mm. 11-12)   7. (m. 5)

6''
7'
11   9'
10
4   6'
4'
7   4'
5
2   4'
9
6   8'
3'
11   4'
10
7

MELODIES

GLOSSARY

Cross-references in the glossary are indicated by **bold face**.

accented dissonance: A dissonance appearing on an accented beat or accented portion of the beat. See also **nonchord tones**.

added-tone chords: **Triads** with one or more added tones, but not the usual **seventh, ninth, eleventh,** or **thirteenth chords**. Typical added tones are the sixth, e. g., C-E-G-A, and the ninth, e. g., C-E-G-D. Added-tone chords are found most commonly in tonal music from the late nineteenth century on.

anacrusis: One or more tones appearing before the downbeat of a measure or **phrase**. Sometimes the effect of an anacrusis, or pickup, is extended over one or more measures.

answer: See **fugue**.

antecedent: See **phrase**.

anticipation: See **nonchord tones**.

appoggiatura: See **nonchord tones**.

augmentation: The expansion of note values in the subsequent appearance of a **durational** pattern; e. g., ♩ ♫ ♩ ♩ is an augmentation of ♪ ♬ ♪ ♪ . The opposite process is **diminution**.

augmented interval: See **interval**.

augmented sixth chord: A **chord** serving a pre-dominant function (see **chord function class**) often containing the **interval** of an augmented sixth between its outer voices and sounding as a major-minor **seventh chord**. In C major, typical examples are the Italian sixth (It. +₆), A♭-C-F♯; the German sixth (Ger. +₆), A♭-C-E♭-F♯; and the French sixth (Fr. +₆), A♭-C-D-F♯.

basic duration: The duration representing the basic pulse of a **meter**, e. g., a quarter note in $\frac{4}{4}$.

binary form: A form consisting of two main parts, with its pitch materials based on one primary melodic unit, often a **motive**. The general plan below is typical of binary forms at the time of J. S. Bach (1685-1750).

$$\|: a \cdots \cdots : \| : \cdots \cdots (a) \cdots : \|$$
$$\quad 1 \qquad (2) \qquad\qquad 1$$

The letter *a* indicates the melodic unit appearing in the principal **tonality**; the numbers indicate tonalities; the parentheses, optional features. The dashes indicate continuation or spinning out of pitch materials deriving from the primary melodic unit. In many cases, the dominant harmony of the principal tonality is achieved at the first double bar, is prolonged for a short while after the double bar, and then gives way to a **return** of the tonic. If the original melodic unit returns where indicated by (a), the form type is said to be *rounded binary*. An important derivation of binary form is **sonata form**.

cadence: A point of repose in a musical passage. In **tonal** music, there are two basic types of cadences, those that imply closure (called *closed* or *terminal*) and those that imply continuation (called *open* or *progressive*). *Melodically*, the cadence type is generally determined on the basis of the relation of the cadence tone (the final tone in the melody) to the prevailing scale and to the triad built on the tonic. If the cadence tone is scale degree 1 or 3, the cadence is felt as closed. Otherwise the cadence is felt as open, with the exception that scale degree 5 may be perceived as part of the tonic chord in some instances.

Harmonically, cadences are classified on the basis of the functional harmonic relationship existing between the cadence chord and the chord immediately preceding it. The standard harmonic cadence types are given below. The Phrygian half cadence iv$_6$-V is more common in the minor mode than in the major, but it may appear in both. Flatting the notes A and D in the other examples will give minor mode equivalents of each cadence type. See also **modal cadences, transient terminal cadence.**

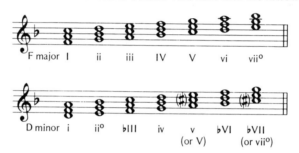

canon: Strict **imitation** carried on for a significant period of time. A familiar example of canon is a round.

chord: A vertical combination of tones, such as a **triad.**

chord function: The role a chord plays in its **tonal** context. Generally, chord function is determinable only in tonal contexts in which the harmonic basis is triadic. This text uses the following notation:

All triads are numbered by their position above the tonic and in relation to a major scale constructed on it. In this way, iii or III will always refer to a triad rooted on the major third degree above the tonic; ♭III will always refer to a triad rooted on the minor third above the tonic, etc. Large roman numerals represent major triads; small roman numerals represent minor triads. A plus sign added to a large numeral denotes an *augmented* triad, e. g., in F major, I$^+$ = F-A-C♯, while a small circle added to a small numeral denotes a *diminished* triad, e. g., in D minor, i^o = D-F-A♭.

chord function class: A term that describes a simplified way to classify the role of a chord in its **tonal** context (see **chord function**). Instead of separate numerals for each chord, chords are grouped by class. In this text, three chord function classes are used: tonic (T), dominant (D), and pre-dominant (P). The table below summarizes the contents of each chord function class. (Note that the pre-dominant class is divided into **diatonic** (d) and **chromatic** (c) types.)

CLASS	MEMBERS
Tonic (T)	I(i), vi(♭VI), IV$_6$(iv$_6$)
Dominant (D)	V(V$_7$, V$_9$, V$_{13}$), vii^o(vii$^o_7$, vii$^ø_7$)†, iii$_6$ (rare)
Pre-dominant diatonic (Pd)	IV(iv), ii(ii^o), ii$_7$(ii$^ø_7$), vi(♭VI)
Pre-dominant chromatic (Pc)	secondary dominants (e. g., V/V, vii^o/V)††, ♭II$_6$, aug.$_6$)
†The symbol ^{ø} means the chord is half-diminished, e. g., B-D-F-A.	
††The symbol V/V means V of V, or II; the symbol vii^o/V similarly denotes iv^o.	

The notion of chord function classes is based on the fact that in triadic **tonal** music, the essential harmonic motion is from tonic to dominant and back to tonic, with pre-dominant chords often preceding the dominant, especially at cadences. Chord function classes are useful as a first step in gaining familiarity with harmonic progressions. For example, the progression I-IV-V-vi-V/V-V-I may be more easily perceived at first as T-Pd-D-T-Pc-D-T. Additionally, chords substituting for tonic or dominant could be symbolized by Ts (e. g., vi) and Ds (e. g., I$^6_4$).

chord mutation: Inflecting a chord member to produce a tone or chord not in the scale in effect, e. g., in C major, flatting the A in the subdominant triad to produce F-A♭-C.

chromatic: A term referring to a **scale** of twelve tones, within an octave, with a half-step between each pair of tones, e. g., C-C♯-D-D♯-E-F-F♯-G-G♯-A-A♯-B. Pitch materials are said to be chromatic if they imply derivation from a chromatic scale.

chromatic third relation: See **third relation.**

coda: A final section of a composition or movement that provides a strong sense of conclusion. In some works, especially those of Beethoven, the coda provides additional **development** of materials. Short codas, often appearing within a movement, are called *codettas.*

composite meter: A meter derived from two **simple** or **compound meters.** Common examples are $\frac{5}{4}\left(\frac{3}{4} + \frac{2}{4} \text{ or } \frac{2}{4} + \frac{3}{4}\right)$ and $\frac{15}{8}\left(\frac{6}{8} + \frac{9}{8} \text{ or } \frac{9}{8} + \frac{6}{8}\right)$. The internal division depends on the grouping of durations within the measures.

composite rhythm: The durational pattern resulting from the combination of patterns of vertically aligned

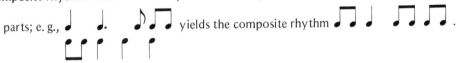

parts; e. g., ♩ ♩. ♪♫♩ yields the composite rhythm ♫♩ ♫♫♩.

compound meter: A meter in which the first level of subdivision of the beat is triple. Common examples are compound duple: $\frac{6}{8}$, $\frac{6}{4}$, etc.; compound triple: $\frac{9}{8}$, $\frac{9}{4}$, etc.; and compound quadruple: $\frac{12}{8}$, $\frac{12}{4}$, etc.

conjunct: A term referring to melodic motion by step.

consequent: See **phrase.**

contrapuntal: Adjectival form of **counterpoint.**

contrary motion: A relationship between voices characterized by pitch motion in opposite directions.

countermelody: A melody, usually of secondary importance, presented simultaneously with the main melody.

counterpoint: The combination of two or more melodic lines, each with independent characteristics. Typical contrapuntal compositions are those which employ **imitation,** especially **fugue.** A more or less equivalent term is **polyphony.**

countersubject: See **fugue.**

cross-relation: The close occurrence of two different inflections of the same note in different voices,

e. g., the F♮ and F♯ in

development: The manipulation of previously presented materials. The most common developmental procedures are fragmentation of a melodic unit, **variation, sequence,** and the introduction of **tonal** ambiguity. See also **sonata form.**

diatonic: A term referring to a **scale** of seven tones within an octave, with five whole-steps and two half-steps. (The sequence of whole- and half-steps differs in each **mode.**) Pitch materials are said to be diatonic if they imply derivation from one of the diatonic modes.

diatonic third relation: See **third relation.**

diminished interval: See **interval.**

°7 and ⦰7: See **seventh chord.**

diminution: The reduction of note values in the subsequent appearance of a durational pattern; e. g., ♩ ♫♫♩ is a diminution of ♩ ♫♫♩ ♩. The opposite process is **augmentation.**

disjunct: A term referring to melodic movement by skip.

Dorian scale/mode: See **mode.**

double stop: On string and wind instruments, the sounding of two tones simultaneously.

duration(al): A term referring to the total time span of a sounding event. Duration is one of the four characteristics of a musical tone. See also **pitch, intensity, timbre.**

dynamics: A term referring to level of loudness or **intensity,** such as forte (*f*) or piano (*p*). When changes in intensity levels are gradual, the term *graded dynamics* is applied. In music where the intensity level changes abruptly, such as the music of the early eighteenth century, the term *terraced dynamics* is often applied.

$\frac{8}{5}$ **sonority:** A sonority containing an octave and a perfect fifth above the lowest tone (allowing doublings

of the tones), e. g.,

eleventh chord: A chord of five thirds formed by adding a third above the ninth of a **ninth chord.** Examples are C-E-G-B♭-D-F and C-E-G-B♭-D-F♯, the latter often called an augmented eleventh ($+_{11}$) chord.

enharmonic: A term referring to different spellings of the same tone or sonority, e. g., F♯ and G♭, or D♭-F-A♭ and C♯-E♯-G♯.

episode: A passage based on previously presented materials, often serving to change **tonality** and to provide contrast. See also **fugue.** (In a **rondo form,** episode is the name sometimes given to the sections which alternate with the ritornello.)

escape tone: See **nonchord tones.**

Fr. +$_6$: See **augmented sixth.**

fugato: A **fugue**-like passage in an otherwise nonfugal composition.

fugue: A type of **contrapuntal** composition employing **imitation** as the chief means of presenting materials. In the initial portion of a fugue (often called the *exposition*), the primary melodic unit of the fugue, called the *subject,* is presented at the tonic pitch level then is imitated at a different pitch level (often the dominant) by another voice and called the **answer.** The alternation of subject and answer statements usually involves as many voices as are present in the fugue. Other elements of a fugue are the *countersubject,* a melodic unit of secondary importance that consistently accompanies subject and answer material; **episodes,** sections in which the subject is incomplete and which serve primarily to change the **tonality;** and various contrapuntal devices such as **pedal point, stretto, inversion, augmentation,** and **diminution.** The concluding section of a fugue generally restores the initial **tonality** and often includes one or more statements of the subject material. Familiar examples are the fugues of J. S. Bach's *Well-Tempered Clavier.* See also **fugato.**

functional harmony: Harmony of the triadic tonal system in which there is a hierarchy of relationships around the tonic, the central **triad.** Typical functional harmonic progressions are I-IV-V-I, I-vi-IV-V, etc. See **chord function** for a description of chord numbering.

Ger. +$_6$: See **augmented sixth.**

glissando: Sliding from one tone or group of tones to another.

ground bass: A melodic pattern, appearing commonly in the bass voice, that is continuously repeated as a background for other musical activities. See also **variation forms, ostinato.**

harmonic rhythm: The rate of change of chord roots.

hemiola: A special case of **syncopation** that momentarily changes the metrical accent from two to three per measure or vice-versa, as in the second measure of this example:

hocket: The presentation of a melodic unit by giving successive fragments (one or more tones) to different voices.

homophony: Essentially a chordal **texture** in which the highest part stands out as the melody (e. g., a chorale), as distinct from **polyphony** and **counterpoint.**

imitation: The successive presentation of a melodic unit in different voices. See also **canon, stretto, fugue.**

intensity: A term referring to the loudness or softness of a tone. Intensity is one of the four characteristics of a musical tone. See also **pitch, duration, timbre.**

interval: The distance between two pitches. In a major **scale,** the intervals between the first and each subsequent scale degree are, in order, M2, M3, P4, P5, M6, M7, and P8 (M = major, P = perfect). Decreasing the size of a major interval by one half-step results in a minor (m) interval. Decreasing the size of a perfect interval by one half-step results in a diminished (o) interval, and increasing the size of a major or a perfect interval by one half-step results in an augmented (+) interval.

inversion: Denotes 1) *chord inversion,* in which a chord tone other than the root stands as the lowest member; 2) *textural inversion,* in which lines exchange their roles (e. g., the bass line is transferred to the soprano and vice-versa); and 3) *melodic inversion,* in which the contour of a melody or a melodic unit is turned upside down.

irregular division of the beat: Divisions of the prevailing beat unit into patterns not common to the meter, such as triplet eighth notes in $\frac{2}{4}$. Irregular divisions also appear at levels above and below that of the beat, e. g., triplet quarter notes or triplet sixteenth notes in $\frac{2}{4}$.

It. $+_6$: See **augmented sixth.**

key: A system of pitch relationships involving a central tone (tonic) and a central sonority (tonic major or minor **triad**), to which all other tones and sonorities are hierarchically related. The terms key and **tonality** are not synonymous, since the former denotes a set of relationships while the latter denotes only a central tone. See also **scale, mode, related keys.**

Locrian scale/mode: See **mode.**

Lydian scale/mode: See **mode.**

Mm$_7$ and mm$_7$: See **seventh chord.**

MmM$_9$ and Mmm$_9$: See **ninth chord.**

major scale: See **mode.**

minor scale: See **mode.**

meter: The measurement of rhythm. See **simple, compound,** and **composite meter.**

Mixolydian scale/mode: See **mode.**

modal cadences: Cadences common to the music composed prior to the appearance of the major-minor tonal system. Typical cadence types are given below. Note that in each instance, the next-to-last chord is rooted on the seventh degree of the **mode.**

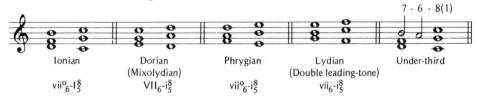

mode: A particular ordering of whole- and half-steps in a **diatonic scale.** All the modes may be reproduced at the piano by playing only the white keys for one octave beginning on the white keys indicated below in parentheses:

Ionian, or major mode (C); Dorian mode (D); Phrygian mode (E); Lydian mode (F); Mixolydian mode (G); Aeolian, or natural minor mode (A); Locrian mode (B).

monophony: A term referring to music consisting of a single unaccompanied line, as opposed to **homophony** or **polyphony.**

motive: A short pattern within a composition. Generally, motives are recognizable primarily by their melodic and/or rhythmic characteristics.

N$_6$ (Neapolitan sixth): A major **chord** built on the lowered second degree of a major or minor **scale.** This chord usually appears with its third in the bass and serves a pre-dominant function (see **chord function class**).

neighbor tone: See **nonchord tones.**

ninth chord: A chord of four thirds formed by adding a third above the seventh of a dominant **seventh chord.** Common examples are the MmM (e. g., C-E-G-B♭-D) and the Mmm (e. g., C-E-G-B♭-D♭). (Often, the fifth of the chord is omitted.) Both types are generally called dominant ninth chords.

nonchord tones: The following examples demonstrate the various types of nonchord tones. Note that *passing tones* and *neighbor tones* may exist singly or in groups of two or more, and that passing tones, neighbor tones, *appoggiaturas* and *escape tones* may appear in accented or unaccented versions. They may also be **diatonic** or **chromatic.**

The *suspension* is an accented nonchord tone, but the preparation of the suspended note and the tie normally associated with the suspension figure tend to lessen the effect of accent. The three stages of the suspension figure—preparation, suspension, and resolution (P,S,R)—are shown in Example 6(a). Less common suspension types—*change-of-bass* and *change-of-soprano* suspensions—are shown in Example 6(d) and (e). Also shown are a *chain of suspensions,* an *ornamental resolution* of a suspension, and a *retardation,* a suspension that resolves upward. Suspensions are numbered by the interval between the suspended note and its resolution above the bass (or below the soprano). Suspensions may be rearticulated rather than tied to the note of preparation and may appear in several voices simultaneously.

Standard abbreviations for the nonchord tones are *p. t.* (passing tone), *n. t.* (neighbor tone), *ant.* (anticipation), *app.* (appoggiatura), *e. t.* (escape tone), *susp.* (suspension), and *ret.* (retardation).

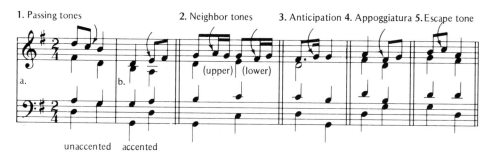

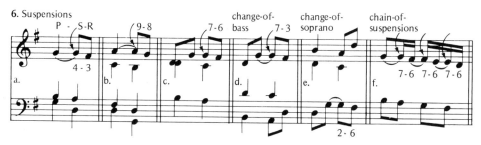

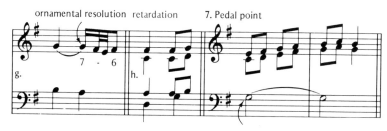

nonfunctional harmony: Harmonic relationships not organized hierarchically in terms of a tonic; the opposite of **functional harmony.** See also **pandiatonic.**

oblique motion: A relationship between voice parts characterized by a lack of pitch motion in one of the parts.

ostinato: A figure of one or more tones repeated continuously for a significant period of time as background for other musical events. See also **ground bass** and **pedal point.**

pandiatonic: A term referring to the relatively equal use of the tones of a **diatonic** scale without a context of **functional harmony.**

parallel major or **minor:** See **parallel mode.**

parallel mode: A mode with the same tonic as another, e.g., G major and G minor.

parallel motion: A relationship between voice parts characterized by pitch motion in the same direction at the same intervals.

passing tone: See **nonchord tones.**

pedal point: See **nonchord tones.**

pentatonic: A term referring to a scale of five tones within an octave that contains a gap of a minor third, e. g., C-D–F-G-A.

phrase: A distinctive pitch unit concluded by a **cadence.** Phrases often are made up of one or more **motives** and are commonly presented in pairs of similar length and structure. In such pairs, the first phrase is called the **antecedent,** the second the **consequent.** The pair together creates a **period.**

Phrygian scale/mode: See **mode.**

pickup: See **anacrusis.**

pitch: The specific frequency of any tone, measured in vibrations per second. Pitch is one of the four characteristics of a musical tone. See also **duration, intensity, timbre.**

point of imitation: A section of a composition based on a single melodic unit presented in **imitation**. In sixteenth-century music especially, the basic material for many compositions consists of several points of imitation, each based on a separate section of the text.

polymeter: The use of more than one meter in a composition or a passage, either *successively* or *simultaneously* in different parts.

polyphony: A texture of two or more distinct but approximately equal lines. See also **counterpoint**.

quartal chord: A chord built of two or more perfect fourths.

quintal chord: A chord built of two or more perfect fifths.

reduction: A process in which a melody, **contrapuntal** passage, or harmonic progression is reduced from its original form to a more skeletal (and usually simpler) version consisting only of emphasized, or basic, pitches.

register: A term referring to portions of pitch span or range of a voice or instrument. On a piano, each octave is a register, while the human voice is often divided into upper (or head) and lower (or chest) registers.

related keys: *Near-related* keys differ by only one accidental more or less in their key signatures. Keys near-related to C major, for example, are A minor, G major, E minor, F major, and D minor. In regard to C major, all other keys are *distantly related.*

relative major or **minor:** See **relative mode**.

relative mode: A mode with the same tones (therefore the same key signature) as another mode, but with a different tonic. For example, C major is the *relative major* of A minor, and A minor is the *relative minor* of C major.

restatement: The repetition of a melodic, rhythmic, or textural passage after intervening materials, e. g., the restatement of the first theme in the recapitulation of a **sonata-form** movement.

return: A general term referring to the reappearance of some aspect of a composition after intervening materials, e. g., the return of the principal **tonality**. A specific kind of return is **restatement**. Return, especially tonal return, is a common principle of most music. See **binary form, ternary form, sonata form**.

rhythm: The recurrence of sound or pulsation. See also **meter, harmonic rhythm**.

rhythmic density: The number of tones per unit of time. Generally, rhythmic density changes during the course of a composition, and these changes help to delineate structure.

ritornello: See **rondo form**.

rondo form: A form characterized by the regular alternation of a principal **section**, sometimes called the *ritornello*, with one or more contrasting sections, sometimes called **episodes**. Here is a typical scheme:

$$A \quad B \quad A \quad C \quad A$$
$$1 \quad 2 \quad 1 \quad 3 \quad 1$$

The letters refer to melodic and rhythmic material and the numbers, to different **tonalities**. The form is typical of final movements in multimovement works, such as sonatas and symphonies, though it also occurs in single-movement works.

root: See **triad**.

root movement: Movement expressed by the interval between chord roots, as a movement by fifth.

running bass: A bass line characterized by continuous movement in one note value, often an eighth note, in works of the late seventeenth and eighteenth centuries. The line serves as harmonic support and background for less active upper voices.

scale: An ordered arrangement of pitch materials into fixed **intervals** within the span of an octave, such as a major scale, a **chromatic** scale, etc. See also **mode, diatonic**.

section: A portion of a movement or work characterized by its relative completeness of presentation of musical ideas. A section is a significant element in overall formal structure. The term is general in that it refers to major divisions of a movement or work as well as to important subparts. The context in which the term is used generally clarifies its meaning.

secundal chord: A chord built of two or more adjacent seconds (major or minor). Secundal chords are sometimes called *clusters*.

sequence: Immediate repetition, generally literal, of a melodic or harmonic pattern at a different pitch level within the same voice. Sequences often consist of three or more statements of the pattern.

seventh chord: A chord of three thirds formed by adding a third above the fifth of a **triad**. Common examples are the major-minor seventh or Mm_7 (e. g., C-E-G-B♭), the minor-minor seventh or mm_7 (e. g., C-E♭-

G-B♭), the diminished seventh or o₇ (e. g., C-E♭-G♭-B♭♭), and the half-diminished seventh or ⌀₇ (e. g., C-E♭-G♭-B♭). The Mm₇ built on the fifth degree of a major or minor **scale** is called the dominant seventh chord.

similar motion: A relationship between voices characterized by pitch motion in the same direction but not at the same intervals.

simple meter: A meter in which the first level of subdivision of the beat is duple. Common examples are simple duple: $\frac{2}{4}$, $\frac{2}{8}$, etc.; simple triple: $\frac{3}{4}$, $\frac{3}{8}$, etc.; and simple quadruple: $\frac{4}{4}$, $\frac{4}{8}$, etc.

sonata form: A form especially characteristic of the first movements of multimovement works (sonatas, symphonies), typically consisting of three main sections, the *exposition, development,* and *recapitulation.* The main features of the exposition are 1) the establishment of the principal **tonality** by a first **theme,** 2) the establishment of a contrasting tonality by a second theme (in some cases the first theme reworked), and 3) a cadence in this second tonality. Other common features of the exposition are a **transition** between the two theme areas, which itself may contain distinctive melodic materials, and a *closing section* or *Codetta* which serves the purpose of bringing the exposition to a strong conclusion. This section, too, may have distinctive melodic features. If the main theme sections contain distinct subsections with individual pitch materials, the term *theme group* is often used.

The *development* section takes its name from its primary purpose—to **develop** previously stated materials. Tonal instability is the rule of this section; several **tonal regions** are usually passed through before the preparation for the return of the principal tonality in the third section, the *recapitulation.* Here the materials of the exposition are restated, usually in their original order of appearance, with tonal adjustments so that the main materials appear within the principal tonality. There often is a **coda** to the movement, and there may be an introduction. Sonata form is a derivation of **binary form.**

sonority type: Any kind of chord, such as a **triad,** a **seventh chord,** etc.

stretto: A type of **imitation** characterized by overlapping entries of the imitated unit. See also **fugue.**

subject: See **fugue.**

suspension: See **nonchord tones.**

syncopation: A conflict with the normal accentual pattern of a meter by means of durational or dynamic accent, e. g., the quarter notes in the second measure of this example:

ternary form: A form consisting of three **sections,** commonly described by the scheme ABA, or ABA . The letters A and B represent distinct sections and pitch materials, though the materials of B may derive from those of A. The prime denotes a degree of alteration, usually in pitch materials, though there may be a change in length as well. The A sections are generally in the same **tonality,** and the B section is either in a different tonality or a different **mode** of the tonality of the A section. Commonly, there is a strong cadence at the end of each section in the tonality of that section, and a **coda** may follow the final section.

tertian chord: Any chord built in thirds, e. g., a major or minor **triad** or **seventh chord.**

tessitura: The general or average pitch level of a vocal or instrumental line, or of a certain passage of such a line; e. g., a line of high tessitura would fall in the upper part of the pitch span or range of a particular instrument or voice.

text setting: The manner in which syllables of text are set to pitch materials. There are three basic types: 1) *syllabic*—one tone per syllable, 2) *neumatic*—two or three tones per syllable, and 3) *melismatic*—many tones per syllable.

texture: A term referring to the number and relationship of individual voices in a composition. See also **homophony, polyphony.**

theme: A relatively complete musical unit, comprising distinctive pitch and rhythmic components, that forms a significant structural unit of a composition. Generally, a theme consists of at least one **phrase,** which is often made up of one or more **motives,** exists within one **tonality,** and concludes with a **cadence.**

third relation: An interval relationship of a major or minor third between two chord roots. If the two chords are both a part of the same diatonic scale, the relationship is **diatonic,** e. g., I-iii, i-III; otherwise the relationship is **chromatic,** e. g., I-III, I-♭III.

thirteenth chord: A **chord** of six thirds formed by adding a third above the eleventh of an **eleventh chord.** The most common type is the *dominant thirteenth chord* (e. g., C-E-G-B♭-D-[F or F♯]-A). In practice, the eleventh (F or F♯) is usually omitted, as is often the ninth.

timbre: A term referring to the tone quality or color of a voice, an instrument, or an instrumental group. The common instrumental timbres are string, woodwind, brass, and percussion, with the timbre of the piano having both string and percussion characteristics.

tonal region: A **tonality** of secondary importance within a composition. Tonal regions are usually transient in nature, appearing commonly in the second section of **binary forms** and in the **development** section of **sonata form.**

tonal, tonality: Terms referring to music with a tonal center. The tone serving as the center is the *tonic.* In triadic tonality, the tonality of the major-minor system, the tonic triad (I or i) is the central harmony. See also **functional harmony.**

tonic: See **tonal.**

transient terminal cadence: A progressive **cadence** in which the cadence chord (or tone) momentarily assumes the role of tonic by virtue of the preceding harmonic (or melodic) activity.

transition: A passage that helps to connect two significant **sections** of a movement. Generally, a transition includes some chromaticism, both to point out its transitional nature and to bring about the change from one **tonality** to another. Frequently, such passages derive their pitch and rhythmic materials from the previous section, though transitions may themselves have distinctive materials. See also **sonata form.**

triad: A **chord** of three members, usually one built in thirds (see **tertian chord**). A typical triad is C-E-G, in which the members, in order, are called *root, third,* and *fifth,* the latter two so called because they form an **interval** of a third and a fifth, respectively, with the root.

variation: A process in which some of the details of a pattern are altered when the pattern is repeated. The alteration may be in any of the pattern's dimensions—pitch, rhythm, etc.—but it leaves intact the essential characteristics of the pattern, its basic pitch shape and/or rhythmic shape.

variation form: A form whose basic structure depends on **variation** as the primary form-building process. There are two main types, *continuous* variation and *sectional* variation. In the former type, the basis for the form might be a recurring bass line (**ground bass,** *passacaglia*) or simply a recurring succession of harmonies (*chaconne*). Such a ground, or **ostinato,** is repeated continuously as a background against which melodic and harmonic elaborations are projected to create the work. In the latter type, often called *theme and variations,* the *theme* is generally a complex of melodic, harmonic, and rhythmic materials cast in a well-defined form (often **binary**). This theme then serves as the basis for subsequent sections which vary in one way or another the details of the theme.

whole-tone: A term referring to a scale of six tones within an octave containing equal intervals of a major second between tones, e. g., C-D-E-F♯-G♯-A♯.

INDEX

Throughout the index, the last number to the right is the page number. Composers' names are abbreviated to the first three letters (for example, *Dun* for Dunstable). In addition, the following abbreviations are used:

A 4
B 5
C 6
D 7
E 8
F 9
G 0
H 1
I 2
J 3

416 07/05 8
44944   BUI